GW00454977

For if the trumpet give an uncertain sound,
who shall prepare himself to the battle?

1 Corinthians 14:8

Cover design by Lawrie Morrisson

Second edition 2018, Hamilton House Publishing Ltd, Rochester Upon Medway, Kent, UK ME2 3EA. First edition published by Hamilton House Publishing Ltd in 2015, www.hamiltonhousepublishing.com.

In association with

ISBN: 978-0-9957205-3-4

Thanks to Peter Currie, Glyn Jarrett, Kirk C. White and Lawrie Morrisson for their assistance and encouragement; to Colombe Anouilh d'Harcourt, Barbara Tesler-Anouilh, Nicolas J. Anouilh and Julie Hamon for permission to quote extensively from *Antigone* by Jean Anouilh; and to the brethren of St Laurence Lodge No. 5511 for their continuing fraternal love.

The opinions expressed in this work are entirely my own. They do not represent the opinions of the United Grand Lodge of England, the Masonic Province of Essex, St Laurence Lodge No. 5511 or any of my brethren. I would like to state quite firmly that this work has no official status whatsoever.

The author, Dr David West, gained his first degree in philosophy from the University of Exeter and his doctorate from the University of Leicester. He taught at universities in England and Canada. He served on government committees on the future of work and was an adviser to a Cabinet (government) Minister. His business career included Ford and Xerox before he founded The Working Manager Ltd, and creating the core of its management education process. His mother lodge is St Laurence No. 5511, and he is a member of several orders beyond the Craft.

Printed in England for Hamilton House Publishing by Biddles Books Ltd, King's Lynn, Norfolk, UK PE32 1SF.

For Jenny, in thanks for fifty happy years of marriage.

Freemasonry is a moral practice. We enable good men to live respected and die regretted.

There are periodic intervals in human experience when the moral life comes under attack. Now is such a time, and we must respond.

We will become a reservoir of social capital, enabling society to preserve the virtue of trust. We will provide a bastion for the virtues in an amoral world, maintaining a community within which the moral life is lived.

In choosing to become a freemason, a man accepts an obligation to live according to the virtues of the order. Such a choice cannot be made lightly.

There is no sense in which a man can say, 'I want to be a freemason but not a good one.'

To be a freemason is to exhibit specific virtues. The most important of these are the three grand principles – brotherly love, relief and truth – and the four cardinal virtues – prudence, fortitude, temperance, and justice.

Managing the Future of Freemasonry

A book of optimism

David West

Second edition

Revised and updated to 2018

Published by Hamilton House Publishing Ltd

We came for ideas, and the search for the meaning behind them. We came to discuss and explore those ideas in an environment of enlightenment which would not only be tolerant of them, but would also challenge us to see ourselves and the world around us in a different, or at the very least in an enhanced way.

Andrew Hammer

Contents

Preface to first edition

The golden years of freemasonry have passed with the departure of a world never likely to return in the lifetime of anyone who might read this book. The world that we face now may seem less than welcoming to the ideals of our order, but I firmly believe that there are still many men in our society hungry for the fellowship and moral meaning that we offer. Our challenge now is to bring our ideals to the attention of a new and different audience. To reach it will require hard work, open-mindedness, creativity, and above all leadership.

How far that little candle throws his beams! So shines a good deed in a naughty world. [1]

I am convinced that a resurgence of masonry is possible. In fact, it is vital to the rebuilding of our society. What I shall say will not always sound optimistic but if we are to rescue our order, we must take an objective look at our problems and the social changes that have caused them. Only by recognising what has brought us to this pass, can we hope to create solutions. We cannot pretend that our problems will simply go away. The optimism that runs through this book depends upon an ability to change.

Preface to the second edition

Only three years have passed since the first edition was published, but a call from booksellers for more copies enabled me to update the examples and figures in the book to 2018, and to correct some infelicities. I was never happy with the chapter on social capital and this has largely disappeared, its text subsumed into other chapters. I have also recognised some hopeful signs following on from what I have called the end of decency, and though these may seem small in the general scheme of things, I have seized upon them.

I have also added a short section on the future. I have no more knowledge than anyone else of what the future holds for our brethren, but I do think we need to think about it.

---

[1] *Merchant of Venice*, Act V, Scene 1.

The membership problem

In late 2014, I received an email from a brother mason I have never met, and who lives 4700 miles away. Despite this, his story resonated.

Last night my lodge in Vancouver had a short memorial service. Of our members, we had a serving militia soldier, a wounded and decorated veteran of the Korean War, and a long-retired militia Major with 21 years' service. Then we held the customary business followed by our annual installation of officers. We had nobody willing to accept office as Deacons or Stewards. The new Director of Ceremonies was absent due to illness. Our Grand Lodge has provided an optional short form for this sort of thing and we used it.

We had about ten members and two visitors present, the latter taking important ceremonial roles. Two past masters also took part but would not accept election or appointment. Neither is a regular attender: one has business commitments, the other lives several hours' drive away, not counting a ferry trip. Everybody was very happy that the meeting was short. Less than an hour for the whole thing, knocks to knocks. We had a little dinner of very mediocre Chinese food after our board meeting and before lodge. After lodge we had a little dessert, coffee and the formal toasts and I was home before 10.30 to the surprise of my wife.

A few years ago we consolidated with another lodge and had about 100 members. We are now down to 32. I am 81 years old, Chaplain in one lodge, Tyler in another and Junior Warden of a third which is going dark in a few days. This is a sad but not unusual picture for Vancouver. Ballooning population and shrinking membership in freemasonry, concordant bodies and everything else: service clubs, lawn bowling, churches, Legion. No one can make any sense of it.

Our current membership problem has existed for more than sixty years, during which time we lost around half our membership. In their important paper published in 2000, Henderson and Belton drew attention to the fact that worldwide masonic membership reached its peak around 1960.[1] At that time there were just over four million freemasons in America. By 2014 American masonry had lost nearly three million members, just over 70% of its membership. In 1950, the United Grand Lodge of England (UGLE)

---

[1] 'Freemasons: an Endangered Species?', Kent Henderson & John Belton, *AQC*, Vol. 113, 2000. The reception it received in *Quatuor Coronati* Lodge was disheartening.

issued 22,500 certificates, a post war peak.[1] In 2017, it issued 6,714. Membership in 2018 is no longer the often quoted 350,000 but nearer to half that figure, and UGLE's decline continues at a rate of about 4/5% per year.

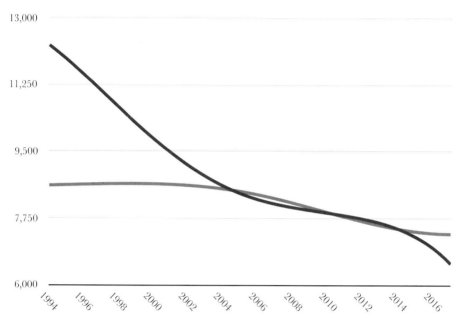

In the graph above, the dark line is the trend of certificates issued by UGLE since 1994, and the lighter line is the trend of the number of lodges. Lodges were able to cope for a time with the decline in certificates (more or less identical to number of candidates) and the number of lodges did not respond to the decline in candidates until about 2003/4, when the number of candidates dropped to 1.0 per lodge. This seems to be evidence for the commonly held view that a lodge needs better than three candidates in two years to prosper. Note that the lines separate again in 2015, indicating the likelihood of more lodge closures.

The second graph *(following page)* shows that the trend of number of candidates per lodge fell rapidly from 1994 to 2004. It steadied for a time but turned down again in 2015.

---

[1] 30,000 certificates were issued in 1920. Paul R. Calderwood, 'Architecture & Freemasonry in 20th-Century Britain', *AQC*, Vol. 126, 2013.

In 2017, there were on average 0.92 certificates/candidates per lodge.[1]

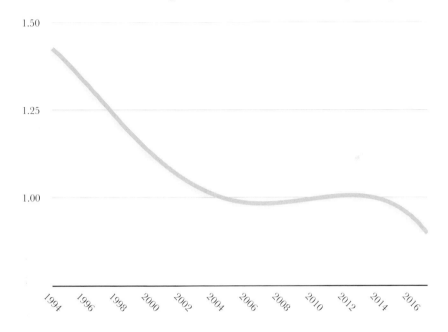

Not just us

It is significant that most organisations similar to freemasonry – those needing regular commitment from their members – reached peak membership around the same time, and each declined in much the same way. This similarity leads one to seek a common cause. [2]

	Year of peak membership	*Decline from peak by 2000*
Jaycees	1975	58%
Lions	1967	58%
Elks	1970	46%
Kiwanis	1960	42%
Rotary	1967	25%

---

[1] *Report of the Board of General Purposes*, 13 December 2017.

[2] US membership figures from *Bowling Alone*, Robert Putnam, Simon & Schuster, 2000.

The plan of the book

We start with an examination of the early years of the nineteenth century, a period which exhibits uncanny parallels with today, and in which 42% of our lodges were lost. Freemasonry almost died as the small trades and crafts disappeared in the Industrial Revolution. Eventually, and I think accidentally, freemasonry found a new source of membership with the blossoming Victorian middle class. Odd as it may seem, given that the period saw two world wars, little changed in the social and moral life of Britain from 1850 to 1950, and the Victorian middle class and its successors sustained masonry for a hundred years. However, during the 1950s a quiet revolution occurred, one which began the end of the middle class. The book studies three distinct periods of this change, each of which had a deleterious effect on freemasonry and institutions like it. These periods caused our decline and formed the society from which we must recruit today.

Trust is central to society and its decline parallels that of masonry. I shall argue that here we find an opportunity to make a contribution to society and an opportunity to save ourselves: to offer a bastion for trust and morality until the wave of barbarism has passed. The book also takes a look at a future; at the automation & artificial intelligence revolution whose effect on employment may be a replica of the Industrial Revolution.

To explain the role I see for our order, I review the philosophical issue of value and examine the absence of ethical principles in today's society. In doing this, I apply Alasdair MacIntyre's account of the virtues to freemasonry. I shall employ the phrase *live respected and die regretted* as a way of approaching Aristotle's notion of the virtues, and use the masonic word *excellences* as a way of handling what might be a surprising idea that there can be many virtues incompatible with each other.

I shall ask what excellences make sense of western society, and follow MacIntyre in arguing that there are none. In the absence of any agreement on what I call the *purpose-to-life*, ethical discussion becomes next to impossible. To resolve this, I will compare our order to the rule of St Benedict, and argue that just as a man may authentically choose to adopt the rule of St Benedict, so he may also choose to become a freemason, the notion of *authenticity* derived from Jean-Paul Sartre. Such a choice is a moral one and I shall argue that freemasonry is a moral order. I shall argue that making the choice to become a freemason provides a meaning to life.

There are many implications stemming from this, one of which is that we must cease to listen to the siren call of PR, and make a positive statement of what we are and what we offer. The book analyses the excellences of freemasonry because we must be clear about those we ask our brethren to sustain. The false gods of PR have sought to change those excellences and so I examine their original meaning, and finally offer some thoughts on the leadership we require.

This is a book of optimism. I believe that we can achieve a resurgence. More than this, I believe that we can become more relevant to society than ever before. I will not say that it will be easy and I recognise that resistance will be strong. Many lodges will fail, but then many always have. There are brethren who would rather see their lodge go dark, as our North American brethren put it, than accept change.

Reading the book

I would like to suggest reading the book one chapter at a time, pausing for reflection after each, if that does not sound too egotistical. Some chapters may be difficult for some readers, especially those which are essentially a matter of moral philosophy. I provide a précis of the argument which I hope will help. If it all becomes too much, I suggest you skip forward to complete the book and come back at your leisure to review the philosophical bits. They may make more sense then.

Freemasonry and social change: 1800–1850

The condition of England

The Napoleonic War left Britain with a large national debt, and the government of the day sought to retain income tax, hitherto a temporary measure. Nicholas Vansittart, then Chancellor of the Exchequer, argued that income tax was progressive, pressing more on the rich and *the least oppressive and the least objectionable of any tax that had ever been imposed.*[1] He was defeated by a huge majority and the burden of taxation shifted to indirect taxes which pressed more heavily on the poor. With no other way of expressing discontent, demonstrations and riots broke out, put down by violent repression as the country became all but ungovernable.[2] 1815 was the *hey-day of aristocratic excess and swagger,*[3] and the political leadership with its cult of amateurism had no understanding of what was happening.

> The King has virtually abdicated; the Church is a widow without jointure; public principle is gone; private honesty is going; society, in short, is falling to pieces; and a time of unmixed evil is come upon us.
>
> Thomas Carlyle, *Edinburgh Review* 1829

Thomas Carlyle described *The Condition of England* as a matter of two nations, the rich and the poor[4] and in 1819, William Cobbett wrote:

> *Society ought not to exist, if not for the benefit of the whole. It is and must be against the law of nature if it exists for the benefit of the few and for the misery of the many … [A] society, in which the common labourer … cannot secure a sufficiency of food and raiment, is a society … whose compact is dissolved.*[5]

In France, that society was dissolved by the revolution which resulted in the execution of Louis XVI and of 40,000 other French men and women.

---

[1] *Parliamentary Debates*, First Series, vol. 33, 1816.

[2] Edward Vallance, *A Radical History Of Britain*, Abacus, 2010.

[3] Sarah Richardson, *The Domestic Impact of the Napoleonic Wars*, University of Warwick.

[4] Thomas Carlyle, a political observer of the French Revolution and its causes, *Chartism*, 1839, republished 2012, Ulan Press.

[5] *Political Register*, September 1819, William Cobbett. A working-class newspaper pressing for parliamentary reform, attacking the rotten boroughs and supporting the Swing Riots.

Whether or not Louis' consort, Marie Antoinette, actually said *Qu'ils mangent de la brioche,*[1] such a sentiment fitted both France and England at the time. During this period, our brethren faced the loss of their traditional livelihoods, a loss not only of employment but also of self-respect and status. Urbanisation meant near-slum living conditions, and the loss of contact with families, becoming a stranger in a strange land. With no money to cushion the change, the risk of poverty and the workhouse was very real at a time when to be poor was to be seen as a criminal. With an almost complete absence of leadership, it is a wonder that the institution of freemasonry did not disappear altogether.

A change in membership?

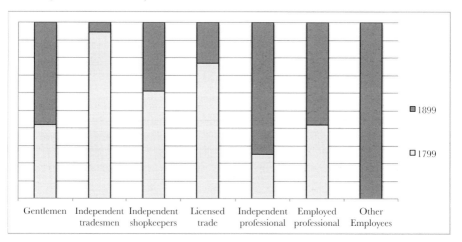

Using data from returns made under the *Unlawful Societies Act* of 1799, this graph displays the change in the employment of members of some Essex lodges from 1799 to 1899. For example, the number of independent tradesmen reduces almost to zero in 1899. In 1799, very few members could be described as employees, and those few included two clergymen, a soldier and an excise officer. By 1899, over half the members were employees, many with jobs unheard of a hundred years before: insurance agent, station master, salesman, broker and advertising agent.

---

[1] Most commentators say not. It was first used by Jean-Jacques Rousseau 35 years before.

The analysis of change in employment in Essex generally accords with David Harrison's analysis of initiates in lodges in Stockport, Warrington, Oldham and Bolton. He writes:

> ... *the foundation on which these lodges were built seems to have been those active in trading the High Street – the shopkeepers (grocers, butchers, bakers, watchmakers). In the first half of the century, the balance of the sector was innkeepers and in the second half the number of merchants and agents rose sharply. It was equally noticeable that the number of industrialists and professionals (solicitors, doctors, clergy, public officials, engineers) rose very sharply in the 1850s ... also noticeable was the decrease in importance of men following a trade ... joiners, farriers, smiths, cordwainers, building tradesmen and ... weavers, spinners, fustian cutters.* [1]

Constructed from Harrison's data. A different categorisation but the same picture: fewer tradesmen and more employees and white-collar workers.

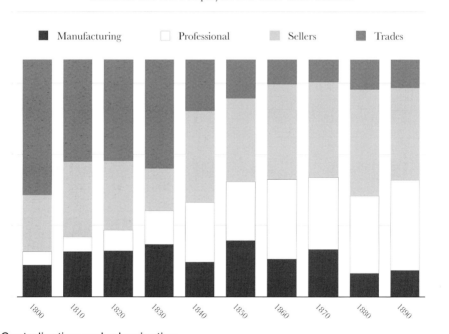

■ Manufacturing   □ Professional   ▨ Sellers   ▨ Trades

Centralisation and urbanisation

Occupations in the eighteenth century had been much the same as in the seventeenth but the industrial revolution changed all that – and at a faster

---

[1] David Harrison, *The Transformation of Freemasonry*, Arima Publishing, 2010.

rate in the UK than in other nations. Britain was becoming the workshop of the world, producing finished goods so efficiently that it could undercut locally made products in almost every country.[1] The immediate effect of the industrial revolution was to move production from the cottage to centralised, mechanised production facilities, driven initially by water power and later by steam. Industrialisation brought urbanisation.[2] London's population doubled between 1801 and 1850. The Manchester and Salford conurbation grew from 25,000 in 1772 to nearly half a million in 1851. At the turn of the century, 1.4 million people (28% of the workforce) were employed in manufacture and mining. By 1841 that figure had more than doubled to 3.3 million (41% of the workforce).[3]

The impact on masonic membership

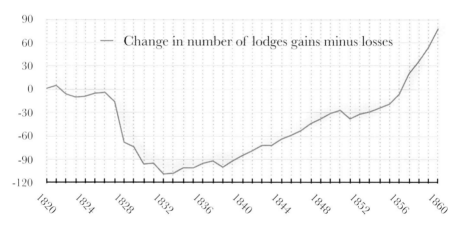

Within the life expectancy of a man born in 1780, traditional jobs, the livelihoods of at least two-thirds of our brethren, virtually disappeared. Disruption was on a grand scale, with a consequent impact upon our order. Between 1820 and 1860, some 252 lodges under the United Grand Lodge of

---

[1] Paul Kennedy, *Rise and Fall of the Great Powers*, Random House, 1987.

[2] In 1820 the City of London was linked up by *an almost continuous line of houses with Hammersmith, Deptford, Highgate and Paddington. For London, like other English cities, had always grown outwards, not upwards.* G. M. Trevelyan, *History of England*, Longman, 1973.

[3] B. R. Mitchell, *British Historical Statistics*, Cambridge University Press, 1988. There was an increase in the speed of industrialisation around 1830 which coincided with an increase in the number of lodges lost.

England were lost, 200 of these between 1820 and 1840. To put this into perspective, 252 lodges represented 42% of the total number of lodges that existed at the 1832 renumbering.[1] The trough in the number of lodges continued until 1840; not until 1857 did we regain the 1820 number.[2] It was not as if our brethren left a blacksmith's forge and moved seamlessly to a skilled job in a factory, earning more money and living a better life. Brethren were forced out of their trade by mass manufacture that undercut their prices and they had to leave home to find what they could in the nearest town. Finding another lodge to join was not the first thing on their minds.

After the Napoleonic war, prices fell by an average of 0.2% a year.[3] Lower prices did not benefit our brethren because they were matched by a greater decline in wages. In the building trade, wages fell 7% in 1825, staying at that level for another 15 years.[4] The working class has almost never been able to put something aside for a rainy day and such a reduction in wages must have been painful. The only employment category that showed wage growth was that of clerks, more than doubling their earnings between 1797 and 1861.

Around the turn of the century, nearly one person in ten was receiving poor relief and that surely included many of our brethren. The loss of a job, failure of an employer's business, illness or accident could lead families to a slippery slope, at the bottom of which lived the really poor. Movement into poverty was easy enough, but getting out next to impossible. Steven King speaks of the ample evidence that:

> ... between 1750 and 1850 both the scale of the poverty problem and its intensity increased. More people became more poor ...[5]

Charles Dickens

The novels of Charles Dickens (1812–1870) may be full of wonderful

---

[1] The list of lodges was closed up seven times.

[2] The data refers only to lodges meeting in England. John Lane, *Masonic Records 1717-1894*, United Grand Lodge of England, 1895.

[3] Deflation continued, on and off, until the advent of the 1914–1918 war.

[4] Data B.R. Mitchell, *op. cit.*

[5] *Poverty and welfare in England 1700–1850*, Manchester University Press, 2000.

characters but they are also political tracts in their depiction of the squalid conditions of the poor,[1] and the descent into poverty of middle class men and women is a theme in many of his novels. He often rescues them by use of the artificial device of an inheritance; artificial because Dickens recognised that in real life poverty was usually a permanent state. Dickens himself was haunted by poverty and his own education had been affected by his family's financial troubles. As Simon Callow said:

> *The reason I love him so deeply is that, having experienced the lower depths, he never ceased, till the day he died, to commit himself, both in his work and in his life, to trying to right the wrongs inflicted by society … From the moment he started to write, he spoke for the people, and the people loved him for it, as do I.*[2]

Oliver Twist (1838) gives us the horrors of Jacob's Island. No creation of the author's imagination, it was on the south bank of the Thames, east of St Saviour's Dock in Bermondsey. Once a wealthy centre for the timber trade, jobs became scarce when the trade started to move down river in 1811. During the cholera outbreaks in the middle of the nineteenth century, half the deaths occurred on Jacob's Island. Despite the increase in national wealth brought by the industrial revolution, average life expectancy at birth had risen by only five years to forty years by 1850, due to the

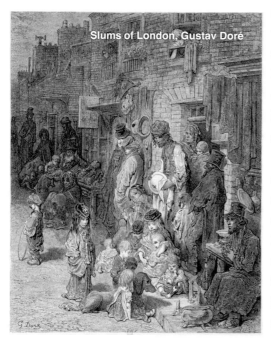

Slums of London, Gustav Doré

---

[1] The discovery (July 2015) of annotated copies of the magazine *All the Year Round*, edited by Dickens, shows that he was the author of passionate articles on the mistreatment of the poor. His attack on the *demented disciples who push arithmetic and political economy beyond all bounds of sense* has some resonance today.

[2] *The Guardian*, 4 February 2012.

dreadful conditions that the urban poor endured.

With the great influx of people, any accommodation in London was ruinously expensive and Jacob's Island was just the worst of many slums. The rich considered the poor a different race. In 1844 Wilberforce[1] preached:

> We look ... every Sunday at our well-filled churches, and we forget, for the moment, in the presence of those we see, the multitudes we see not; whose misery, as well as sin, whose want of room, want of clothes, indolence, neglect or utter wretchedness, are shutting out from our fellowship, and severing from civilisation and religion ... In all our great towns, thin walls separate luxury from starvation. The two classes live in absolute ignorance of each other: there are no points of contact between them ... selfish respectability degrades one set, whilst misery and recklessness, which soon turn to vice and wickedness, weigh down the other.

In 1820, the legislation governing poverty in England and Wales was still the 1601 Poor Law. Under this law, *charitable relief* (compare our use of the word in *brotherly love, relief and truth*) was administered by the parish in which an applicant could claim rights, by residence, birth, marriage or apprenticeship. Such relief, which might include food and clothing as well as money, was known as *outdoor relief.* The cost of such relief was levied on wealthy, and usually unwilling households and the cost increased dramatically in the first half of the industrial revolution. The wealthy sought to reduce the tax by arguing that relief should not be given to the 'undeserving poor'.[2]

They argued that poverty was a matter of bad habits: drinking, gambling and idleness. To mollify the wealthy, the 1834 Poor Law Amendment Act sought to stop outdoor relief, directing that the helpless poor should be sent to what became known as the workhouse, where conditions were deliberately made so miserable that only the desperate poor would seek relief. The word *workhouse* induced fear even in my grandmother, and she died in 1971.

While some workhouses were properly operated, many starved their inmates

---

[1] Bishop Samuel Wilberforce, *Charge*, 1844. Known as 'Soapy Sam', he was the son of the great anti-slavery reformer, William Wilberforce.

[2] Terry Pratchett wrote that *while it was regarded as pretty good evidence of criminality to be living in a slum, for some reason owning a whole street of them merely got you invited to the very best social occasions,* in *Feet of Clay*, Corgi Books, 2013.

to death. Joshua Hobson's 1848 report on the Huddersfield workhouse shows:

>...*that the sick poor have been most shamefully neglected; that they have been and still are devoid of the necessary articles of clothing and bedding; that they have been suffered to remain for weeks at a time in the most filthy and disgusting state; that patients have been allowed to remain for nine weeks together without change of linen or of bed clothing; that beds in which patients suffering in typhus have died, one after another, have been again and again and repeatedly used for fresh patients, without any change or attempt at purification; that the said beds were only bags of straw and shavings, for the most part laid on the floor, and that the whole swarmed with lice ...*

I have cut short this horrifying description but in truth Huddersfield was not the only example of such evils. After the 1834 Amendment, there was a reduction in the number of able-bodied men seeking relief, if only because the workhouse was an effective deterrent.[1] Karel Williams has argued that the 1834 *Amendment* at least offered at least a safety net for many in need, during the immense changes in society.[2] This may be true, but in practice outdoor relief continued, based upon the recognition that few of the poor were really undeserving and that poverty had always threatened a large percentage of the population.

During the banking crisis of 1796/7, when the land bubble burst and the Bank of England was forced to suspend the exchange of gold for banknotes, 40% of households in the village of Ardleigh in Essex were pauperised, and

>... *up to one-third of any birth cohort from the early eighteenth century onwards would expect to come into contact with the poor law at some point ...*[3]

Social unrest

The 1789 French Revolution was initially an inspiration. Richard Price, a member of the Royal Society, who died just two years after the start of the revolution, was inspired to write:

---

[1] Crime increased during this period. In the Black Country, theft increased by 188%.

[2] *From Pauperism to Poverty*, Routledge and Kegan Paul, 1981.

[3] King, *op. cit.*

Why are the nations of the world so patient under despotism? Why do they crouch to tyrants, or submit to be treated as if they were a herd of cattle? Enlighten them and you will elevate them. Shew them they are men and they will act like men. Give them just ideas of civil government and let them know that it is an expedient for gaining protection against injury and defending their rights, and it will be impossible for them to submit to governments little better than contrivances for enabling the few to oppress the many. [1]

and Wordsworth wrote. [2]

Oh! pleasant exercise of hope and joy!
For mighty were the auxiliars which then stood
Upon our side, we who were strong in love!
Bliss was it in that dawn to be alive,
But to be young was very heaven!

Thomas Paine, who had motivated the war of independence in America, now supported the revolution in France with his *Rights of Man* (1791) and the government of the day, led by Pitt the Younger, became worried. The response was legislation, not to help the poor but to enable force to be used against any signs of revolution in England. 1792 became known as the *annus mirabilis* of radicalism, a year in which George III found it necessary to issue a Royal Proclamation *Against Seditious Writings and Publications*.

Famously in 1799, Pitt brought in the Unlawful Societies Act *for the more effectual suppression of societies established for seditious and treasonable purposes*. The Act called for a list of names, occupations and addresses of all lodge members to be sent annually to the Justices of the Peace[3] and, as Glyn Jarrett has pointed out, it must have had an impact on the membership of freemasonry.

It is not easy to isolate that impact but the experience of the London Corresponding Society (LCS) is indicative. Founded by a shoemaker Thomas Hardy and much influenced by Thomas Paine's *Rights of Man*, its membership, once as many as 80,000, was drawn from those disenfranchised

---

[1] *A Discourse on the Love of our Country*, The Constitution Society, 1789.

[2] *Prelude.*

[3] The Act was not repealed until 1967 although dead letter for some time.

by the electoral process. In 1794, the leaders of LCS and other groups were indicted for high treason, and three were sent for trial. All were acquitted, but members were seriously frightened. LCS never recovered.

The fight against mechanisation

Our brethren faced alarming disruption in their working lives, a constant fear of poverty, poor working conditions and a reduction in wages. Attempts to resist in ways quite normal today, such as public meetings or strike action, were put down, frequently in a brutal manner. For example, the productivity of wheat farming consistently increased over the period and, with an consequent oversupply of labour, wages fell. They had already been reduced to seven shillings and workers were threatened with a further reduction to six. This led to the formation in 1832 of the Friendly Society of Agricultural Labourers who refused work for less than ten shillings a week.

The men met at Tolpuddle in Dorset. A local landowner invoked the 1797 *Unlawful Oaths Act*, which prohibited people from swearing oaths to each other[1] and which had been designed to prevent naval mutinies, such as those at Spithead and the Nore. James Brine, James Hammett, George and James Loveless and Thomas and John Standfield were found guilty and sentenced to transportation to Australia. Happily 800,000 signatures meant that in 1836 the Tolpuddle Martyrs returned. Loveless wrote:

> *God is our guide! from field, from wave,*
> *From plough, from anvil, and from loom;*
> *We come, our country's rights to save,*
> *And speak a tyrant faction's doom:*
> *We raise the watch-word liberty;*
> *We will, we will, we will be free!* [2]

Attempts to prevent mechanisation and its inevitable effect on wages, were as useless in 1832 as they had been earlier under the leadership of Ned Ludd, General of the Army of Redressers. The Luddites had sought to prevent the

---

[1] Distinct from the *Unlawful Societies Act of 1799*, although with a similar purpose.

[2] *Victims of Whiggery* 1837, in *The Uses of Poetry*, Denys Thompson, Cambridge Univ. Press, 1978.

installation of power looms and frames in the wool and cotton trades. After the 1812 *Destruction of Stocking Frames Act*, protest incurred the death penalty.

> Byron was one of the few who spoke out against the Act and the repression of the working men who sought to call attention to their plight. In the House of Lords he said: *When a proposal is made to emancipate or relieve, you hesitate, you deliberate for years, you temporise and tamper with the minds of men; but a death bill must be passed off hand without a thought of consequences.*

The real Ned, if he ever existed, was long dead[1] but one of the many letters written over his name read:

> ... *we won't only pray but we will fight, the Red Coats shall know when proper time's come, we will never lay down our arms till the House of Commons passes an act to put down all the machinery hurtfull to the commonality and repeal that to Frame Breakers – but petition no more, and that won't do, fighting must.*

The first half of the nineteenth century came closer to revolution than any time since the 1642 civil war. Some of the disturbances included:

1816	*Spa Fields* Islington, for electoral reform and relief from poverty.
1817	*Pentrich March*, against unemployment and food prices.
1819	*Peterloo Massacre*, a murderous reaction to a Manchester pro-reform meeting; 750 cavalry, 600 infantry, two six-pounder guns and 400 constables killed 500 peaceful people, women seemingly targeted.[2]
1820	*Cato Street Conspiracy*, an attempt to form a radical government by blowing up the Cabinet.
1820	*Swing Riots*, agricultural workers destroying threshing machines, led by the fictitious Captain Swing.
1831	*Reform Bill Riots*, against rejection of the Reform Bill in the Lords.
1838	*Chartists*, seeking secret ballots and votes for all men over 21.

Political reform

To the ordinary man in the street, including our brethren, it must have seemed that the whole world was in flux: massive changes in the nature of

---

[1] An Edward Ludd around 1779 in Leicester is said to have broken stocking frames, although the stories of Ned Ludd are fictional.

[2] The Mike Leigh film *Peterloo* features my wife! Only as an extra it is true, but ...

work, movement from country to city, protests and social unrest, extreme poverty combined with extreme wealth. Faced with a similar situation, France experienced four dictatorships, three republics, two monarchies and two empires from 1789 to 1914. Britain, with more enlightened Tory and Whig governments, eventually enacted a succession of measures against entrenched interests. This reduced the pressure driving unrest, and in time, legislation achieved everything that the French Revolution sought.[1] Nevertheless, in the meantime, Britain suffered from leaders with feet of clay.

Absence of leadership

George IV (regent 1811, king 1820–1830) was obese, addicted to opium and

oblivious to what was going on away from his court. Victory in the Napoleonic Wars had been gained without his involvement or, it seems, interest. He was far more taken up with fashion; one of his favourites, Beau Brummell (1778–1840), claimed to take five hours to dress and to have his boots polished with champagne.

1820, the year of George's coronation, was more notable in the public mind for his attempt to divorce his estranged wife, Queen

---

[1] As Tory Home Secretary, Sir Robert Peel established the Metropolitan Police Force in 1829 with a thousand constables. In the same year, under the Duke of Wellington, the Tories brought in the Catholic Emancipation Act. The 1830–1834 Whig government brought in the great Reform Bill of 1832, abolishing most of the rotten boroughs and providing further enfranchisement. They also restricted the employment of children with the first of the Factory Acts in 1833, brought in the Slavery Abolition Act in the same year, and amended the Poor Laws in 1834. Prime Minster for a second time in 1841, Peel extended the Factory Acts and repealed the Corn Laws which had prevented the import of corn from abroad. The repeal divided the Tories and Peel resigned. The Whig government under Viscount Melbourne enacted Municipal Reform (1835) to establish local government elected by ratepayers and further reduce the rotten boroughs.

Caroline, using a parliamentary bill to show that she was guilty of adultery. The debate was salaciously reported by the newspapers of the day, the King claiming that he and the Queen never had sex after the second night of the marriage and that he had *to conquer* [his] *aversion and overcome the disgust of her person*. In response, the Queen claimed that her husband was so drunk that he spent most of the wedding night in the fireplace, *where he fell, and where I left him*. The populace was firmly on the side of the Queen and celebrated when the bill was withdrawn.

The absence of leadership shown by the King was reflected in freemasonry. Lodges can do quite well on their own, up to a point, but there is always a need for central leadership to administer, educate, inspire, reward and advise. During periods of great change, great leadership is required, but was not forthcoming. I will take three provinces as examples and examine the involvement of their Provincial Grand Masters (PGMs) and the regularity of meetings of Provincial Grand Lodges (PGLs). Such meetings are not significant in themselves but their occurrence is a useful indication of the involvement and commitment of the PGM and the Provincial Executive.

The Essex experience

Keith Buck reports[1] that in 1814 there were fifteen lodges in Essex. By 1832, there were four. In 1815, the PGM, William Wix, presided over what seems to have been a successful meeting of PGL, the minutes of which indicate a decision to hold future meetings twice a year. No further meetings occurred, and in 1823 Wix resigned, leaving the county to live in Kent. His deputy left in the same year. The next PGM, William Honywood MP, was offered the position in 1824 but delayed acceptance until 1828, accepting only when a deputation of Essex masons invited him to make a decision on the spot. His installation never took place; a sick man, he died in 1831. His deputy had been appointed in 1827 but did very little either and moved away in 1832. In effect, there was no PGM between 1823 and 1836 when Rowland Alston was appointed, with one son as his deputy and another son as Provincial Grand Secretary, although the two did not overlap in office. Whether such nepotism

---

[1] Keith S. Buck, *Provincial Grand Lodge of Essex 1776–1976*, privately printed 1976.

was right or wrong, at least some leadership was available to a province which had received none since 1815.

The Lincolnshire experience

The story of the province of Lincolnshire is much the same. The Revd William Peters had been PGM from 1792 until his death in 1814 but appears to have played no part in the life of the province.[1] As William Dixon writes: *Lincolnshire provincial records show scarcely any attendance on the part of PGM.*[2]

He was followed by William Henry White,[3] described by Dixon as:

> … *an entire stranger* [who was] *never installed, never attended a meeting and never interfered or took any interest whatever in the province.*

The Revd Matthew Barnett had been a founder of the first lodge in Lincolnshire in 1787, and was appointed Deputy PGM in 1793. He continued in office for another forty years by when he must have been getting on for 80. With the best will in the world, it is difficult to conceive how anyone at an advanced age, born before the industrial revolution took hold, could provide leadership in the middle of massive social and economic changes, entirely on his own. As Dr George Oliver reports:

> *Neither Bro. Peters nor Bro. White ever held a Provincial Lodge in my time.*[4]

That is true enough. For twenty-one years, 1793 to 1814, there were only seven meetings of PGL, and none after 1806. (Oliver was initiated in 1801.) From 1815 to 1826, a period of fourteen years, there were just three, all after White had left the county. No more meetings were held until 1832, when the next PGM, Charles Tennyson d'Eyncourt, was installed.

He had been appointed six years earlier but, in keeping with the times, seemed in no hurry to organise his installation. Thereafter, meetings were

---

[1] He was also Deputy Provincial Grand Master of Nottinghamshire; held five or six 'livings' and was a popular portrait artist who charged 80 guineas a time (about £8,000 today.)

[2] *Freemasonry in Lincolnshire*, William Dixon, Forgotten Books, 2014 (first pub. Williamson 1894.)

[3] Not the Grand Secretary of the same name.

[4] From his oration after receiving a *testimonial & a silver cup and service of plate contributed to by Freemasons in all parts of the world* in 1844. *The Builder*, December 1919.

held almost annually from 1832 to 1859. How much of this was due to the PGM is an open question, for Dixon writes: *His speeches on the rare occasions when he presided at PGL were eloquent and interesting.* No doubt the Lincolnshire masons would have preferred that his attendance was usual and his speeches inspirational. Oliver wrote of d'Eyncourt's[1] management:

> *Masonry during this time declined so much there was scarcely an efficient Lodge in the province; the Barton, Grantham, Grimsby and Sleaford Lodges had entirely discontinued their meetings. Even the Lincoln and Boston Lodges were feeble.*[2]

During d'Eyncourt's period, Lincolnshire experienced zero growth of lodges but the opportunity of new membership was there if there had been leadership to grasp it. Lincoln was lit by gas in 1828; Clayton & Shuttleworth started making steam engines in 1842; the railway arrived in 1846. In 1800 the population of Lincoln was 7,000. By 1900 it was 50,000.

The Sussex experience

Contrast d'Eyncourt's record, as reported by Dixon, with that of Colonel James McQueen who on becoming Deputy PGM of Sussex in 1854 showed that he had thought about leadership: *Let me crave your indulgent consideration on the difficulties that attend my position ... Having sustained a lapse of twenty-seven years without assembling ... had it not been for the unceasing and zealous exertions of several energetic and worthy members of the Craft ... our Grand Lodge might not have continued ... I stand before you a stranger, sensible of the difficulties which beset my path and desirous to the best of my ability zealously and impartially to carry out the duties of my office. The first step I have to take is, I fear, one that may lay me open to misconception, and an imputation of partiality, viz. the appointment of officers, as I deem it prudent to surround myself with brethren long known to me for their zeal ... Let us consider this year as one of probation, in order that we may fairly relaunch our long-stranded Institution, unruffled by waves of anger or envy, and united in the strongest bonds of brotherly love ... and as we progress... I shall be better able ... to select brethren from other Lodges.*

The Province of Sussex had managed to double its number of lodges between 1810 and 1830 and then lose the gain in half that time. Its story is another of absentee landlords, the most obvious being the Duke of Richmond. For the whole of his tenure, he was abroad in Ireland, Brussels and Canada, where he had been appointed Lieutenant Governor and where

---

[1] A snob who added his last name to appear to be of noble blood. He also rebuilt his home to look like a castle. His nephew was the poet. Charles was suitably infuriated when the latter became Alfred, Lord Tennyson. He eventually succeeded in gaining a baronetcy for himself.

[2] Oliver, quoted by Dixon, *op. cit.*

he died, having been bitten by a rabid fox. Even had he been active in the affairs of the Province, he may not have been of much use. He was:

> ... *buttoned up tight about affairs and scarcely communicative ... Everything is done by interim secretaries.*[1]

His successor, appointed in 1823 after another delay of four years, was his son[2] who held just one PGL meeting in 1827:

> ...[when] *it would appear that it was intended that the PGL should assemble triennially but, strange to say, no meeting was held for 27 years.*[3]

One of the Sussex deputies was living abroad due to ill-health and on his death, no replacement was made for nine years.

Figurehead or leader?

It is little wonder that so many lodges went under, even if private lodges did make valiant efforts, including the Angel Lodge who in 1834, their hundredth year, initiated James Webb, wonderfully described by Buck as: ... *the ugliest man in Brightlingsea [and] an indefatigable mason. He ... was said to walk to Colchester and back for Lodge meetings, a round trip of twenty miles.* Grand Lodge obviously saw a PGM as nothing more than a figurehead, which seems to contradict Kearsley's view that following the Union:

> *Provincial Grand Masters were [then] required to hold regular meetings at least once a year and to appoint officers.*

They certainly did not, and Kearsley's description of the pre-Union status of PGMs before the union – that they were *appointed in somewhat whimsical fashion* – remained true. The lack of leadership was not limited to Essex, Lincolnshire and Sussex. According to John Armstrong,[4] Sir John Grey Egerton, PGM of Cheshire, 1810-1825, had also *greatly neglected his duties.*

---

[1] Frances G. Halpenny & Jean Hamelin, *Dictionary of Canadian Biography*, Vol. 5, Univ. Toronto Press, 1983. Entry by George F.G. Stanley, quoting Bishop Plessis, Archbishop of Québec.

[2] A brave soldier, severely wounded in 1814, (the musket ball in his chest was never removed) he was ADC to Wellington, MP Chichester 1812–1819, Privy Council 1830, Postmaster General 1830–1834, Lord Lieutenant of Sussex 1835–1860.

[3] Thomas Francis, *History of Freemasonry in Sussex*, Forgotten Books, 2013, (first pub. 1883.)

[4] *History of Freemasonry in Cheshire*, 1901.

Lodges in the provinces wanted leadership, and felt forced to take action when Provincial Grand Masterships were vacant, or when those appointed were absent, dilatory or just bored. Freemasonry figured low in the priorities of the PGMs chosen by Grand Lodge. To use Charles Tennyson d'Eyncourt as an example, he was MP successively for four constituencies, a Privy Councillor, an Equerry to the King, high steward of Louth, Deputy Lieutenant of Lincolnshire, fellow of the Royal Society and a magistrate. Dixon wrote:

> [The] Right Worshipful Brother would have made a most excellent Prov. G. Master had he, in the words of the Old Charge, 'been resolved against all politics.'

The Duke of Sussex

Shelley was never given to understatement but it is hard to entirely disagree with what he wrote after the Peterloo Massacre:

> An old, mad, blind, despised, and dying king,
> Princes, the dregs of their dull race, who flow,
> Through public scorn … [1]

The Duke was a complex and contradictory character. The sixth son and ninth child of King George III, his early adult years were spent abroad. Until 1806 he was rarely in England and it was in Rome in 1792 that he met and married Lady Augusta Murray. Just before their first son was born, the King declared their marriage void.[2] In 1831, after Lady Murray had died, he married Lady Cecilia who was never recognised as Duchess, although achieving some recognition later by Queen Victoria. Money was difficult. The Duke espoused liberal political views which did not please his father nor the later King William IV, and he did not receive the well-paid sinecures Royal Princes normally held.[3] Notwithstanding this, he sought the public eye.

---

[1] Poem 'England 1819', in *Percy Bysshe Shelley*, poems selected by Fiona Sampson, Faber and Faber, 2011.

[2] Under *The Royal Marriages Act*, 1772, the King could veto all Royal marriages until the royal person reached the age of 25. The act was brought in because both William, Duke of Gloucester and Henry, Duke of Cumberland married commoners.

[3] He received just the £18,000 government grant, equivalent to about £2 million today. Under William IV, he was made a Ranger of a Royal Park.

Fulford reports[1] the Duke's excursion to Howick from Newcastle to lay the foundation stone of a new library, at a time when there was little canvassing except during elections:

... the massive figure of the Duke of Sussex, standing up in his carriage beaming and bowing as he drove through a blaze of blue and orange, scandalised and frightened the Tories who were sourly peeping at him out of their windows.

When the 1832 Reform Bill appeared to be in danger in the House of Lords due to Tory opposition, he went to King William IV at Windsor to argue that the necessary number of Whig peers be created to ensure the bill's passage.[2] The King was furious and refused to see the Duke again.[3] For this and for his marriages, he was seen as the least important of the Royal Family, which must have been hurtful. This was a great pity because the Duke was interested in science and the arts. President of both the Royal Society and the Society of Arts,[4] he had a library of fifty thousand books and laid the foundation stone of the University of London.

---

[1] Roger Fulford, *The Royal Dukes: the Father and Uncles of Queen Victoria*, Collins, 1973. A more detailed account of the event, the booze-up of the century, can be found in Gareth Davies, 'The Duke of Sussex lays a Foundation Stone,' *The Square*, June 2015.

[2] Ultimately, Lord Grey and Robert Peel, from opposing parties, combined to get it through.

[3] William IV, third son of George III, never expected to become king. He was a freemason and saw active service in the Navy, eventually retiring as a Rear Admiral under Nelson. The Duke's inability to get on with him says more about the Duke than the King. William was easy-going and informal, ready to use public transport and even offering the government the use of Buckingham Palace when the Houses of Parliament were burned down.

[4] Which became the *Royal Society for the encouragement of Arts, Manufactures and Commerce* in 1908.

He enjoyed singing and amazed a lady who congratulated him on his voice, saying: *I have the most wonderful voice that was ever heard – three octaves.*[1]

He stood *6 foot 3 inches tall and was corpulent by any standards*.[2] He suffered from asthma for the early part of his life and later developed cataracts which required an operation, a new process – dangerous but successful. Towards his end, he suffered from a bacterial infection of the skin, a condition similar to cellulitis. He treated it with turtle soup and orange ices, and died in his bed in 1843. At his own request, he was buried in Kensal Green cemetery, and not with the Royal Family at Windsor. His second wife was buried beside him.

His leadership

Described in contradictory terms as tolerant, liberal, intellectual, autocratic, hands-on, vain, eccentric and wayward, a contemporary wrote of him:

> [It] *would overstate his abilities to say he is a first rate man … intellectual resources not above mediocrity … speeches remarkable for the ardent love of liberty … excels at putting obvious truths into popular form … makes his views as clear to others as they are to his own mind … no one yet mistook the drift of his argument.*[3]

The picture is of someone intelligent enough but not brilliant, self-opinionated, perhaps uncreative, pompous and a poor listener with a liberal conscience. Sandbach writes of his:

> *… progressive inegalitarian outlook … a highly developed sense of his own position … a liking for autocratic power, wielded with a firm but generally courteous hand.*

Masonic writing about Royal masons all too easily becomes hagiography. The truth about the Duke seems to be that despite his success in forcing through the Union with his brother, Prince Edward, Duke of Kent and Strathearn, he lacked day-to-day leadership skills, being given to over-attention to detail and the use of edicts which often, if not usually, rebounded on him. His time was divided among his many interests and freemasonry was not the most important of them. Indeed, he seemed not to take it seriously.

---

[1] Fulford *op. cit.*

[2] Yasha Beresiner, 'Robert Crucefix, a man and a mason to be proud of', *250th anniversary celebrations of Burlington Lodge*, 2006.

[3] R.S.E. Sandbach, 'Robert Thomas Crucefix 1788-1850', *AQC*, Vol. 102, 1989.

When the idea arose of inviting Robert Owen, the social reformer and founder of the cooperative movement, to become a freemason, he replied:

No, by all that is good, were he to witness our ceremonies he would make us all to appear fools. His subjects are of a character too serious and extended for him to be occupied with our trifling amusements.[1]

He allowed himself to be caught up in minor matters: the design of a jewel for the stewards of the Boys' and Girls' Institutions; a committee to revise the RA ritual which, predictably perhaps, came to little. Kearsley's analysis[2] of the priorities of Grand Lodge post-union seems to indicate he had little awareness of the real world. Re-decorating lodge rooms, renumbering lodges, agreeing rank and regalia and arranging a new coat of arms, all these were no doubt amusing but smack of fiddling while Rome burned. Kearsley argues that charity jewels were developed during his Grand Mastership but unfortunately the charities were the pivot of the conflict between the Duke and Robert Crucefix. Some commentators take the view that he opposed Crucefix's creation of the *Asylum for Aged and Decayed Freemasons* because he had not initiated it, but Kearsley writes:

The Duke felt that it would encourage men to join freemasonry for the charity they would get out of it … He thus strongly opposed the idea.

The Duke may well have been right that his scheme of annuities would have been more effective than spending on a building, but creating a win/lose is always a bad way to manage. Facilitating an agreement would surely have been his best contribution. Seeking relief for brethren, and for distressed men and women outside freemasonry, would have focused the order on what was happening in society and given it a relevance it clearly lacked. The Duke surely did not need the continued and silly squabbles between Antients and Moderns but he did not handle these with any tact. His autocratic response to the would-be Antient rebels led to the formation of the breakaway Grand Lodge of Wigan, which kept the Antients' ceremonies alive as recently as 1913. Neglect on the part of yet another Provincial Grand Master was a part

---

[1] Jasper Ridley, *A Brief History of the Freemasons*, Robinson, 2008.
[2] Mike Kearsley, '1814 – Consolidation and Change', *AQC*, Vol. 127, 2014

of the cause.[1] What brethren need in times of great change, then as now, is help in understanding what is happening and advice on what to do about it. In the Duke's situation, more openness and explanation in decision-making was required. The need for a different approach to leadership was clearly seen in the popularity of Crucefix's *Freemasons' Quarterly Review*. That publication, much to the Duke's displeasure, provided a speedy account of what went on in Grand Lodge, publicised the activities of those orders beyond the Craft,

Bernard Cornwell's historical novels[2] are always a good read but he does give his heroes anachronistic opinions and motivations. In the same vein, I may be justly accused of anachronism in arguing that the Duke's leadership style was inappropriate. Autocracy was no doubt the normal mode of behaviour at court and the Duke was no different from any other royal personage. Nevertheless, autocratic commands are usually dysfunctional, especially when they are transmitted through failing local management.

> *The Duke was getting old, his illnesses were prolonged and painful, … his veteran advisers had all passed away … The Grand Master was a changed man; he was hectoring, unjust, despotic; it was not a pleasant sight. Though many fine things were said of him at his passing, his demise brought relief to the fraternity.*[3]

A perfect storm

The impact of the social and economic changes was almost fatal. The time our brethren faced could have turned as bloody as it had in France, with:

- Mechanisation causing a loss of skilled trade livelihoods.
- A change in the nature of work from owner/tradesman to employee
- Rapid urbanisation bringing near-slum conditions.
- A reduction of earnings and a constant fear of the workhouse.
- Legislation against joint action by workers, protest harshly put down.

---

[1] Harrison, *op. cit.*

[2] In addition to his acclaimed *Sharpe* novels, his Arthurian trilogy: *The Winter King, The Enemy of God* and *Excalibur*, is to be highly recommended.

[3] P. R. James, 'The Grand-Mastership of HRH The Duke of Sussex, 1813–1843', *The Collected Prestonian Lectures 1961–1974*, Lewis Masonic, 1983.

All this occurred with an almost complete lack of leadership at all levels. In the 1800s, there was an enormous gap between rich and poor, and senior brethren were among the rich. Charles Tennyson d'Eyncourt was the sole beneficiary of his father's legacy of 2,000 acres. The 5th Duke of Richmond owned Richmond House in Whitehall, Goodwood House in Sussex and vast estates in Scotland. 'Wealthy' William Wix lived in Lloyds House on Bishop's Down near Tunbridge Wells, a house worth maybe four or five million today.

> *In the neighbourhood of Bishops Down, a new Park has been commenced, called Nevill Park, the situation of which for building, has been happily chosen. It commands a most charming prospect, and its short distance from the chalybeate springs, renders it a particularly desirable residence for those who wish to derive benefit from the waters. There is a pleasant walk through this park from Bishops Down to Rusthall Common , and four handsome houses are erected here. One of them ... is at present the residence of Lord Viscount Nevill. The gardens belonging to it are arranged with most exquisite taste, and form a perfect bijou. The views from all parts of the park are varied and extensive, and at each entrance is a remarkably pretty lodge, the rustic appearance of which harmonises well with the surrounding scenery.* [1]

The 'top brass' [2] of freemasonry were isolated from the situation of the ordinary mason, and either could not or would not offer leadership. As the membership that had sustained freemasonry since seventeenth century disappeared, it seemed freemasonry had come to an end. Freemasonry had walked blindfold into a perfect storm. Recovery took place but only as an accident. We are about to find that history has repeated itself – and it should be unnecessary to state that we cannot rely on serendipity once more.

> *Those who cannot remember the past are condemned to repeat it.* [3]

---

[1] *New Guide for Tunbridge Wells,* John Colbran, 1840.

[2] As John 'Lord' Stonely always called them.

[3] George Santayana, *Reason in Common Sense*, first published 1905, Collier Books, 1962.

Freemasonry and social Change: 1850–1950

Recovery

What saved our order was advent of a new source of membership around 1850. The middle class identity, *a clearly defined consciousness based upon the notions of respectability and self-help* as Richard Brown[1] puts it, found an echo in the ideals of masonry. Then in 1874, the popular Albert Edward, Prince of Wales, became Grand Master and made freemasonry fashionable. Lord Brooke, later the fifth Earl of Warwick, became Provincial Grand Master of Essex in 1882.[2] Buck writes:

> *Lord Brooke inspired the Province with … vigour and élan and annual meetings often became gay social occasions much enjoyed by the brethren and their ladies.*

Inspired? Quite the opposite of earlier Provincial Grand Masters.

The Victorian middle class

To understand the middle class and its disappearance in modern times is to understand our membership problem. The Victorian period was not only the most innovative technological time in British history, it also made startling improvements in literacy, medicine, education, democracy and the press. For many people, Victorian buildings still represent the best of our public architecture. Donna Loftus writes of:

> *… the massive expansion of local government and the centralised state, providing occupations for a vast strata of civil servants, teachers, doctors, lawyers and government officials as well as the clerks and assistants which helped these institutions and services to operate.*[3]

Between 1881 and 1911 the number of doctors doubled, the number of government clerks trebled, the number of scientists quintupled, and *for every new solicitor or barrister there were two new legal clerks.*[4]

---

[1] *Change and Continuity in British Society 1880–1850*, Cambridge, 1987.
[2] And later Deputy Grand Master under Albert, Prince of Wales.
[3] *The Rise of the Victorian Middle Class*, BBC History, 2011.
[4] Simon Gunn & Rachel Bell, *Middle Classes: their rise and sprawl*, Cassell & Co, 2002.

Suburbia

The Victorian middle class carved out new areas for itself, progressively moving away from the city centre into suburbia. Its suburban villas, built from the 1860s on, were not just places to eat and sleep. The historian, Francis Thompson, writes that it was there that:

> ... *the family could distance itself from the outside world in its own private fortress behind its own garden fence and privet hedge and yet could make a show of outward appearances that was sure to be noticed by the neighbours, that the suburban lifestyle of individual domesticity and group-monitored respectability could take hold.*[1]

Popular at the time was the writing of Samuel Smiles, particularly his *Self Help*.

> *The spirit of self-help is the root of all genuine growth in the individual ...*

Smiles expresses great admiration for character and argues that:

> *Character consists in little acts, well and honourably performed; daily life being the quarry from which we build it up, and rough-hew the habits which form it ... Mind without heart, intelligence without conduct, cleverness without goodness, are powers in their way, but they may be powers only for mischief.*

I have found no evidence that Samuel Smiles was a freemason and it is unlikely that his writing affected the late nineteenth century ritual books. Any similarity with the ritual may just be evidence of a close accord between Victorian and masonic values.

The Victorian villa housed the middle class values of thrift, respectability, responsibility and self-reliance and the railways took these values further and further afield. Commuting is not a 20th-century invention. The railways grew rapidly from 1825. By 1840 there were nearly 1,500 miles of track and by 1860 the mileage had increased to over 9,000.[2]

Civic involvement and aspirations

The middle class had disposable income. Dr John Heaton, who moved into a Leeds suburban villa in 1856, wrote in his diary[3] of his home improvements, his family's musical evenings, his children's parties and excursions. His relationship with his wife was one of loving domesticity, although much of his

---

[1] F.M.L. Thompson (ed), *The Rise of Suburbia*, Leicester University Press, 1982.

[2] Peak mileage of 20,500 miles arrived in 1927, after which the railways almost fatally declined under Beeching's egotistical misuse of statistics in the 1950s.

[3] Brian & Dorothy Payne, *Extracts from the Journals of John Deakin Heaton, M.D. of Claremont, Leeds*, Publications of the Thoresby Society, Miscellany 1973, Vol. 15.

time was spent outside the home, at work but also in civic engagements. He was a member of the Yorkshire Education and the Leeds School Boards and President of the Leeds Philosophical and Literary Society. He belonged to the Leeds Conversation Club and the Leeds Improvement Society, the latter campaigning for a College of Science and for a Town Hall. He speaks of the achievements of the Leeds Art Gallery with pride.

In the 1880s, the entire income of a working-class family would be about £78 per year. The male earner in families who could afford to be neighbours of the Heatons had an income of more than three times that, and his income was increasing year on year. The Victorian middle class had money for cultural and aesthetic aspirations which, in their minds, went along with moral education. Part of the Victorian middle class self-image was being seen as a professional person and new professional bodies appeared around this time: the Society of Teachers in 1846, the Institute of Actuaries in 1848, the Chartered Banker Institute in 1875, the Institute of Chemistry in 1877 and the Institute of Chartered Accountants in 1880. These bodies gained a Royal Charter soon after their foundation. Membership conferred respectability, and becoming a freemason did much the same.

Philanthropy

Although a later and more cynical age has cast doubt on the motivations of Victorian philanthropy, what cannot be doubted is its extent. Melvyn Bragg reported that the amount contributed to charities in aid of the poor exceeded government expenditure on what is today known as welfare. Such charity work was overwhelmingly Christian. Bragg writes:

> *The theory that poverty is the result of a lack of will and virtue, that indolence and sluttishness and drunkenness and crime render you undeserving of help until you take the path of reform through religion is now, in most of the English-speaking world, spoken of, if at all, with a shake of the head or with contempt for those misguided Victorian days. [This] does not detract from the determination and the faith of those women who with broom, scrubbing brush and pail and the King James Bible, went into the sewers of society on a mission to save souls by way of mending and redirecting ruined lives.* [1]

---

[1] *The Book of Books: the radical impact of the King James Bible, 1611-2011*, Hodder & Stoughton, 2011.

Victorian philanthropy took many guises. The Metropolitan Association for Improving the Dwellings of the Industrious Classes sought to build homes for the poor. In what it called *five percent philanthropy*, the movement asked wealthy donors to invest money at a below-market rate of return, and they did. The Cooperative Movement, almost destroyed by incompetence in 2011, started in Rochdale, Lancashire in 1844. Angela Burdett-Coutts, advised by Charles Dickens, funded the Columbia Market in 1869. She also funded churches, schools, housing schemes and even drinking fountains for dogs, as did John Passmore Edwards, who made his money through newspapers: *The London Echo*, *Building News* and *Mechanics Magazine*. Active in movements for the abolition of capital punishment, the suppression of the opium trade and political reform, he endowed the Whitechapel Art Gallery, the London School of Economics and Political Science, and twenty-four libraries around London, and in Cornwall where he was born.

Later Victorian employers built their own model (meaning *ideal*) villages to house their workers: Bournville, Birmingham (1893) was built by the Quaker Cadbury brothers; Port Sunlight *(above)* in the Wirral (1899) by the Congregationalist William Lever. The Cadbury brothers created a pensions

31

scheme, a workers committee and an employee medical service while William Lever provided an open-air swimming pool, an art gallery, schools, a concert hall and allotments. The total amount donated to charity in 2011/12 is estimated at £9.3 billion; a £2.3 billion decrease compared with the previous year in real terms. In £sterling there is more charitable giving today than in Victorian times, but then Britain today is immeasurably richer and there are a lot more people. If one makes allowance for inflation, population and GDP, the Victorians seem to have been around twenty times more philanthropic than people today.

The salaried middle class

While members of the early Victorian middle class had largely consisted of what we might today call the *upper* middle class, as time went on the label of middle class became associated with the salaried white-collar workers who followed their predecessors out, and further out, into the suburbs. They worked harder for their status, leaving at home not ladies managing servants, but full-time housewives.

House prices actually fell in the 1920s and 1930s; a typical semi-detached in Middlesex cost about £700; one further out £450. In 1935, mortgage repayments would have been 25% of income for a clerk like Bob Harper *(left)*, first Master of my mother lodge. In the 1920s, the long frock coat of the Victorian period gave way to the morning suit, worn by many masons today, but while the financial standing of salaried middle class men would have in no way equalled that of Dr Heaton, their values were much the same.

They were courteous and civil but reserved. Etiquette, manners and dress mattered a great deal; moral rectitude was important and moral respectability even more so. Frugality and temperance became virtues as did limitations on what could be discussed in polite company: no politics, no religion, no money, and definitely no sex.

The sociable 1930s

The Caravan Club reached its pre-war peak in 1939 when 201 outfits turned up for a rally in Northampton. Cycling clubs date from the 1890s but bicycles were recognisably modern by the 1930s. Victor Silvester won the first World Ballroom Dancing Championship in 1922, and contract bridge dates from the 1920s. In these years, a more sociable middle class appeared, holding to the Victorian virtues but more relaxed about them. Social histories of the period speak of whist drives, dances and musical activities organised by local residents' associations. There were tennis, cricket, cycling, amateur dramatic and motor clubs in addition to activities based on the many church denominations. The Ladies' Festival was a major, and expensive, event.

Measured in terms of baptisms per thousand live births, the Church of England baptism rate makes an allowance for changes in population and birth rate and is thus a useful measure of minimal religiosity: attendance at church at least for *hatches, matches and dispatches.* 70% of live births were baptised in this period, actually an increase in religiosity from 1900 to 1930 and most children went to Sunday School. Middle class men would have responded immediately to the charge after initiation:

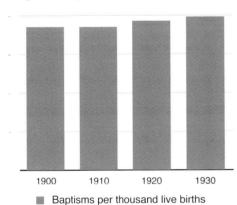

Baptisms per thousand live births

As an individual, I would further recommend the practice of every domestic as well as public virtue. Let prudence direct you, temperance chasten you, fortitude support you and justice be the guide of all your actions.

Very middle class sentiments, in fact.

The true gentleman

Cardinal Newman's description of the true gentleman in his 1852 *The Idea of a University*, captured at least the self-image of the Victorian male and may have partly created it. He writes that the true gentleman:

> ... *is tender towards the bashful, gentle towards the distant, and merciful towards the absurd; he can recollect to whom he is speaking; he guards against unseasonable allusions, or topics which may irritate; he is seldom prominent in conversation, and never wearisome. He makes light of favours while he does them, and seems to be receiving when he is conferring. He never speaks of himself except when compelled, never defends himself by a mere retort. He has no ears for slander or gossip ... and interprets every thing for the best. He is never mean or little in his disputes, never takes unfair advantage, never mistakes personalities or sharp sayings for arguments ... He has too much good sense to be affronted at insults, he is too well employed to remember injuries, and too indolent to bear malice.*[1]

Such a description would have fitted very nicely (in the sense of *exact*) with the self-image of the Victorian, Edwardian and even later freemason. It would not have fitted men in the society that followed.

Now gone away

As a recruitment source, the middle class could not have been bettered. By 1911, there were 900,000 white-collar workers and by 1951, two and a half million, increasing from 5% to 11% of the workforce. Freemasonry was seen as part of the establishment and middle class men aligned themselves with it for that reason. We must now recognise that the middle class, as we have known it, has gone away.

---

[1] *Newman Reader*, The National Inst. for Newman Studies, 2007.

Social change post 1950: overview

In 1950, the Grand Master was probably murdered. Edward William Spencer Cavendish, 10th Duke of Devonshire, died of a heart attack at age 55 while being treated by John Bodkin Adams, a probable serial killer.[1] The next Grand Master, Roger Lumley, 11th Earl of Scarbrough, took the stage with little preparation.

1820s	Today
Mechanisation causing loss of skilled trade livelihoods that in many cases went back for generations.	Downsizing, increased use of IT, the end of the clerical worker. Management redundancies.
Change in the nature of work from owner/tradesman to employee with a loss of self-respect and status.	The end of middle class careers, managerialism, increase in women entering the workforce.
A rapid urbanisation bringing a poorer quality of life with the ever present risk of descent into the slums.	Greater commuting distances, longer hours without pay, working families needing benefits, food banks.
A rash of jobs that were often temporary as companies grew, moved or went under.	1.3 million people underemployed. Zero-hours contracts, part-time work, more 'self-employment'.
Uncertainty and reduction of earnings with a fear of the workhouse; the poor seen as criminals.	Reduction in benefits, worsening terms and conditions. Poor as 'scroungers'. Fear of redundancy. End of company pensions.
Increasing gap between rich and poor. The poor out of sight with protests being harshly put down.	Increasing gap between rich and poor. Unions no longer a force to protect working people.
Social unrest, civil disobedience and fear of revolution, legislation against joint action.	Attacks on trades union, reduction of employment protection, protest marches.

The similarities between the 1820s and 2018 are uncanny. The conditions of the pre-Victorian era seem to have been repeated. Just as then, pay levels for ordinary folk in the UK have declined – by over 5% in real terms between 2007 and 2015. In 2018, younger workers in between eighteen and twenty-one are paid 16% less than they were in 2008.[2] In the years following the banking disaster, the UK was alone in seeing wages decline while the economy grew. One in five workers took a pay cut.[3]

In 2018, 1.8 million people were on zero-hours contracts. 65% of employees

---

[1] More than 160 of Adams' patients died in suspicious circumstances.

[2] London School of Economics' Centre for Economic Performance (CEP).

[3] 2014 *British Social Attitudes Survey*.

said that the amount of work they were expected to do had increased. 34% said that they were expected to work unpaid overtime.[1] A 2018 report, using figures from the Office for National Statistics, showed that almost five million people worked an average 7.4 hours a week without pay. The report estimated that workers lost a total of £31 billion in pay.[2] A 2017 *Global Workforce Study*, conducted by Willis Towers Watson, found that less than half of UK employees had trust and confidence in the job being done by their organisation's leaders.

The one-nation Toryism of the 1950s, and the social democracy of the 1960s seemed to lead towards a more egalitarian and caring state, but such decency was soon replaced by greed. In the 1800s, an *aristocratic excess and swagger* caused a disgust of leadership. A similar level of disgust has been caused in later years by the discoveries of dishonesty within the finance industry, expenses fiddling and cash-for-access in parliament, sex crimes among media personalities and too many other sins against decency to mention. The establishment had shown that it cannot be trusted.

Most of the men that we have sought to recruit and retain have had less time, less money, less energy and less security. Brethren have been unable to commit *to regular attendance at the Lodge of Instruction* because they simply have not known from day to day what demands their employers would put on them. These changes have gone along with other uncertainties resulting from changes in religious belief and the role of the sexes. Reversing the failure of leadership in 1820, it falls upon today's masonic leadership to help brethren through these changes.

1950 to the present

I shall consider the period from 1950 to 2018 in three phases. The first, *The end of rules*, concerns the flowering of social democracy and the primacy of the individual. From the mid-1950s to the 1970s, there was a rejection of the establishment, including almost every cow previously held sacred, including freemasonry. It was a delayed reaction to the privations of WWII, occurring

---

[1] *YouGov*, 2014.
[2] TUC report, coinciding with their *Work Your Proper Hours* Day.

only when prosperity returned. When it did, the Prime Minister Harold Macmillan announced *most of our people have never had it so good.*

The second phase, *Show me the money,* was a reaction to the first and a partly successful attempt to turn back the clock. The title is from the 1996 film *Jerry Maguire.* Anything but one-nation Toryism, there was a meanness about the years from 1980. Its focus on money, an outcome of Thatcherism, was not an environment in which freemasonry could flourish. Brotherly love, relief and truth do not fit with greed and self-interest.

These vices were not what Margaret Thatcher intended to create but they do typify the third phase, *The end of decency.* If the idealism of the 1960s and 1970s seemed to be leading towards a more caring world, the counter-revolution from 1980 onwards, and particularly from 2000, created a vacuum in the moral life. In these three phases lie the reasons for the decline in freemasonry – and in the third phase an opportunity for its renaissance.

Phase one – The end of rules: 1950–1970

As Callum Brown has remarked:

> *... the 1950s was in fact a deeply old-fashioned era, so old that it has often been described as the last Victorian decade.*

Intoxicating times

Good or bad, the main effect of this period was the loosening of the rules and structures that had governed Britain since the rise of the middle class in the 1850s. Some of this was deliberate, for example the introduction of social democracy, and some of it was unforeseen, like rock 'n' roll.

Bill Haley and the Comets

Looking back on this decade from 60 odd years on, when so many of our brethren had not even been born, it is important to emphasise what a dramatic change it was. Jazz had its earthy rhythms and young girls had long swooned over bobby soxers, but in rock 'n' roll there was not only a beat but a revolution. Its early lyrics expressed barely disguised sexual desire but its later lyrics became fused with the protest movement, gaining a powerful political content. Poetry had often been political, as in Wordsworth's fascination with the French Revolution, but the poetry of *the old sheep of the Lake District*[1] was not driven by a pounding electric bass guitar.

To live through *the end of rules* was an intoxicating experience which gave hope for a new world, but it was not one in which an autocratic, structured, hierarchical and Victorian order like freemasonry would thrive. Nevertheless, there were exciting dreams to be part of. Everywhere, everything held such promise of a better and fairer world. Globalisation at that time meant global friendship and understanding, not manufacturing companies chasing ever lower rates of pay. There was a revolution in values, a new emphasis on individual freedoms. Above all, there was a rejection of the old establishment, of *the man* and of *law 'n' order*. There was a wave of frustration and even anger against what had gone before. Graffiti on the garden wall of a doctor's surgery near where I lived read *Smash the hierarchy!* in dark paint that took many years to fade.

A new order appeared in working life and control was rejected in favour of engagement of the spirit. Rank no longer implied knowledge, and the process known as organisational development (OD) sought to break down hierarchical decision-making and to build an organisational life fuelled by interpersonal trust and collaboration. Part of this revolution was feminism which began to change relationships and the use of time.

Just desserts

Harold Macmillan, British Prime Minister from 1957 to 1963, may have been a patrician Tory but he was also MP for Stockton-on-Tees, a depressed northern industrial and market town.[2] The working class had suffered since the depression in 1932, something which Supermac, as he was known,

---

[1] As Rumpole fondly called him in John Mortimer's novels.

[2] It served from 1961 to 1983 as the seat of Bill Rogers, one of the gang of four founders of the short lived Social Democratic Party. The seat was later abolished.

understood. With his one-nation Tory[1] beliefs, he made full employment his aim and his comment about never having it so good was justified by an improving economy, the end of rationing, and an observable increase in living standards.[2] What followed was an idyllic and indeed idealised time, its essence being *whatever turns you on*, and that did not always mean drugs. Do your own thing; be your own person free from external and what seemed at the time to be meaningless rules, as long as you do not cause harm to others. Abbie Hoffman summed this up in his views:

> *I believe in the redistribution of wealth and power in the world. I believe in universal hospital care for everyone. I believe that we should not have a single homeless person in the richest country in the world. And I believe that we should not have a CIA that goes around overwhelming governments and assassinating political leaders, working for tight oligarchies around the world to protect the tight oligarchy here at home.*[3]

President Johnson with Dr Martin Luther King at the signing of the Voting Rights Act, 1965.

---

[1] Stemming from Disraeli, one-nation Toryism holds that one part of society cannot move forward at the expense of another. Special duties fall on the rich; indifference to the suffering of the under class causes instability in society and makes revolution more likely.

[2] The economic success was based on overseas trade: earnings from exports and overseas investments. This consumer demand, but companies failed to make productivity and overseas marketing investments with the result that wage inflation took hold.

[3] Quoted by John T. McQuiston in his obituary of Hoffman, *New York Times*, April 14, 1989.

In the USA, Lyndon Johnson, President 1963–1969, managed to put through his Great Society legislation: an attack on poverty, ending segregation and extending civil rights, welfare and education as well as subsidies for the arts. In Britain, Harold Wilson (1964–1970 & 1974–1976 followed by Callaghan to 1979) legalised abortion, decriminalised homosexuality, abolished capital punishment, extended the Race Relations Act, and introduced equal pay legislation and the Employment Protection Act with maternity leave.

Change in culture

Major theatrical events took place in the late 1950s and 1960s. John Osborne's *Look Back in Anger* came to the stage in 1956, and Arnold Wesker's trilogy (*Chicken Soup with Barley*, *Roots* and *I'm Talking about Jerusalem*) followed from 1958. In films, *Billy Liar* (with Tom Courtenay) came out in 1959, *Saturday Night and Sunday Morning* (with Albert Finney) in 1960, *The L-Shaped Room* (Leslie Caron and Tom Bell) in 1962 and *This Sporting Life* (Richard Harris) in 1963, all demanding change. The 1960s also saw the rise of satire, with *Beyond the Fringe* and *That Was The Week That Was*. The magazine *Private Eye* was first published in 1961. The Aldermaston marches organised by the Campaign for Nuclear Disarmament were a foretaste of the student protests in 1968. Unlike the 1830s and 1930s, the marchers and the protestors were not drawn from the dispossessed. 80% were white-collar workers and professional people.

The change was celebrated at events that have become legendary. *The Summer of Love* hit LA in 1967, the same year that the Beatles released *Sergeant Pepper's Lonely Hearts Club Band*. Their 1966 *Revolver* has been described as the distillation *of an LSD trip into a three-minute song*.[1] Woodstock 'happened' in 1969. Environmentalism was born.

The twenty-year-long Vietnam war aroused widespread rejection of the military-industrial establishment, which President Dwight Eisenhower (Supreme Commander of the Allied Forces in Europe during World War II) warned against in his 1961 farewell address to the nation:

---

[1] *Rolling Stone* magazine.

In the councils of government, we must guard against the acquisition of unwarranted influence, whether sought or unsought, by the military industrial complex. The potential for the disastrous rise of misplaced power exists and will persist.

The war had begun as a Vietnamese battle for independence from France and ended as American paranoia over creeping communism. As a vehicle for dissent, nothing came near it. The critic Charles Marowitz wrote of the 1968 London production of the rock musical, *Hair*:

Without Vietnam and the American repugnance to that war, the show would never have come into being. It is almost entirely nourished by the current generation's hatred of what its 'senior citizens' have allowed America to become.[1]

Public opinion gradually hardened and by 1967 two-thirds of Americans thought the war a mistake. *Make love, not war* for a while replaced *my country, right or wrong* and flower power was the peaceful response to the violent attacks on those who opposed the war. If you were going to San Francisco, you were advised to wear a flower in your hair because *you're gonna meet some gentle people there*.[2] In 1973 Richard Nixon ended American involvement.

Change in management philosophy

The manufacturing theories of Frederick Taylor (1856–1915) and of French mining engineer Henri Fayol (1841–1925) in business administration, stemmed from the 1920s and both were about top-down control. Taylor assumed that workers were incapable of rational thought and that intelligent people (like Taylor) were required to analyse the best way to do a job of work, and instruct workers in minute detail how to do it. Taylor instructed the workers in Bethlehem Steel's pig-iron plant, that:

When [the manager] *tells you to pick up a pig and walk, you pick it up and walk, and when he tells you to sit down and rest, you sit down. You do that right through the day. And what's more, no back talk.*

He explained that workers had just enough brain to be trained, that the:

---

[1] '*Hair* at the Shaftsbury', *Plays and Players Magazine*, November 1968.
[2] First released by the Mamas and the Papas in 1967.

... workman who is best suited to handling pig iron is unable to understand the real science of doing this class of work. He is so stupid that ... he must consequently be trained by a man more intelligent than himself into the habit of working in accordance with the laws of this science before he can be successful.[1]

Henri Fayol famously said that it was the job of management to *plan, organise, direct, co-ordinate and control.*[2] He argued for one single controlling mind to generate a plan for all to follow; that the right to give orders and the power to exact obedience must be vested in management and that the formal chain of command must run seamlessly from top to bottom of the organisation.[3] The views of Taylor and Fayol were treated as common sense through to 1950, and were still the basis of much indifferent management practice in 2018.

Organisational development

Business management changed in the 1960s. One cause of this was the increase in higher education. In a seven year period, the number of men and women graduating annually from UK universities doubled to more than 50,000. There was a proportionately larger increase in the number of higher degrees awarded.[4]

In the 1960s and 1970s, the practice of OD was led by Warren Bennis,[5] Bill Reddin[6] and Robert Blake,[7] and offered a new world of work. The OD practitioners were psychologists, unlike Fayol and Taylor who were engineers. Bennis saw that existing management methods rarely solved problems because the organisation followed established routines which did not get to the underlying issues. He set out goals of change as:

---

[1] Frederick W. Taylor, *Principles of Scientific Management*, Harper & Brothers, 1911.

[2] 'Administration industrielle et générale', *Bulletin de la Société de l'Industrie minérale*, 1918.

[3] Compare this with John Lewis who state: *Our democratic network of elected councils, committees and forums gives Partners* (employees) *a real say in our decision-making processes, and allows us to challenge management on performance and have a say in how the business is run.*

[4] *Education: Historical statistics, Standard Note: SN/SG/4252*, 2012, Paul Bolton, House of Commons Library.

[5] *Organizational Development*, Addison Wesley Longman, 1969.

[6] *Managerial Effectiveness*, McGraw-Hill, 1970.

[7] with Jane Mouton, *The Managerial Grid: The Key to Leadership Excellence*, Gulf Publishing, 1964.

Creating an open, problem solving climate throughout the organisation.

Recognising the authority of knowledge and competence as opposed to rank.

Getting decision-making and problem solving close to the information sources.

Building trust throughout the organisation.

Maximising collaborative efforts.

Increasing a sense of ownership in the workforce.

Growing self-control and self-direction for employees.

Douglas McGregor[1] *(right)* showed that the way managers manage is related to their view of human beings. Some managers take the view that people dislike work and will avoid it if they can; that they must be coerced to put in the required effort, offered inducements and threatened with punishment. McGregor called this *Theory X*. Other managers see work to be as natural as play and hold that people have a capacity for self-control, that they are self-motivated by self-esteem and achievement, and that few organisations make full use of their employees' abilities. McGregor called this *Theory Y*. The increase in higher education has meant that Y is more relevant to management than X.

The *Human Relations* movement (with its roots in the Hawthorne experiments of the 1930s) was directly opposed to command and control and its new emphasis on delegation and creativity was a heady brew. In the 1960s, it became mainstream and Abraham Maslow[2] *(hierarchy of needs)*, Kurt Lewin[3] *(organisational psychology)* and Frederick Herzberg[4] *(hygiene and motivating factors)* became prophets of management.

---

[1] McGregor, Douglas, *The Human Side of Enterprise*, McGraw Hill, 1960.

[2] 'A Theory of Human Motivation', *Psychological Review*, 1943.

[3] 'Group decision and social change', in Newcomb, T. and Hartley, E. (eds), *Readings in social psychology*, Holt, 1947.

[4] *Motivation to Work*, John Wiley & Sons, 1959.

Increase in personal freedoms

The contraceptive pill was licensed in 1960, the same year in which Penguin published the first unexpurgated version of *Lady Chatterley's Lover.* Opening the famous obscenity trial, prosecution counsel, Mervyn Griffith-Jones, amazingly asked the jury whether the novel was *something you would wish your wife or servants to read.* The question was a watershed: one moment a serious question and the next an object of ridicule. It was as if one era gave way to another within the length of a sentence.

While pre-marital sex was daring in the 1950s, by 2014 only a quarter of the population disapproved.[1] Indeed marriage was no longer seen as the only sexual or loving relationship.[2] In the public consciousness, the gay movement began in 1969 as a reaction to the riots against a police raid in New York City. The first Gay Pride March took place in 1970. Attitudes towards gay relationships changed markedly after the *Sexual Offences* Act of 1967.

Feminism

A signally important phenomenon during the whole of this period has been second- and third-wave Feminism. I discuss this in the first phase, but of course this movement has spanned the whole period and is still developing.

Feminism has roots at least as long ago as the fourteenth century. In my book *The Goat, the Devil and the Freemason,* I mentioned Christine de Pizan (1364–1430), most famous for her attack on the mid-13th century narrative poem, *Le Roman de la Rose,* a pornographic manual of courtly love. Being the daughter of a doctor and a mother of three, Christine de Pizan objected mildly to the unnecessary detail, asking *Doesn't everyone know how men and women copulate naturally?,* but much more to the poem's justification of rape.[3] Mary

---

[1] *British Social Attitudes* 2014.

[2] There remains strong support for monogamy; nearly 90% of the population, a figure consistent since 1983, think extramarital sex is wrong.

[3] Writing at a time when women were not thought of as independently capable beings, she was a phenomenon. She was married off at fifteen. After a short but happy marriage, she was widowed and left with her children, her mother and a niece to look after. Her change of fortune obliged her to *take on a man's responsibilities in the world* as she puts it. She began by copying manuscripts and then started to write, becoming a notable literary figure. Her *Book of the City of Ladies* and *Book of the Three Virtues* enjoyed success well into the 16th century.

Wollstonecraft (1759–1797) is best known for her *Vindication of the Rights of Woman* in which she argued that women were equal to men, but just not given the same educational opportunities. The most famous 20th-century UK feminists were the Pankhurst sisters who campaigned for women's suffrage, achieved in the same year that Marie Stopes published *Married Love,* banned as obscene in America.

Germaine Greer

Feminism is not a new movement but it did not affect male society much until the 1970s with the rise of what has become known as *second-wave* feminism. Germaine Greer *(left)* has argued, in *The Female Eunuch,* that the traditional atomic family demeaned and sexually represses women, treating them rather like eunuchs. Like Wollstonecraft, Greer objects to the way that girls are taught to be submissive.

It is hard to argue that women have not been treated abominably when medical insurance companies in the USA refuse to cover conditions arising from pregnancy, claiming that this is not discrimination because it applies to all pregnant persons, male and female. Nevertheless, having got to grips to some degree with the first two phases of feminism, men were taken aback by the third wave, which looked like pre-feminist behaviour in its:

> … *re-adoption by young feminists of the very lipstick, high heels and cleavage proudly exposed by low-cut necklines that the first two phases of the movement identified with*

male oppression.[1] *Pinkfloor expressed this new feminism when she said, 'It's possible to have a push-up bra and a brain at the same time.'* [2]

Naomi Wolf, best known for her 1991 book, *The Beauty Myth*, said:

> *… I conclude that the enemy is not lipstick, but guilt itself; that we deserve lipstick, if we want it, and free speech; we deserve to be sexual and serious – or whatever we please; we are entitled to wear cowboy boots to our own revolution.*

Men should realise that women do not dress for men but for other women.

Women and work

At one time, women's jobs were seen as temporary: ceasing when marriage brought children. Even as late as the mid-1980s, getting on for half of British people still thought of the man as the breadwinner and women as having a supportive and caring role. By 2012, women formed nearly half the workforce, and 87% of people agreed that women could quite properly choose a career over family duties.

Must women always choose between breaking the glass ceiling or wearing the glass slipper? Christy Krumm says that as a teenager she felt ambivalent:

> *On the one hand, the idea of girl power was exciting and fun. It made me grateful to the generations of women who had fought to give me the right to vote, earn a degree, and make the same salary as my male colleagues. Yet, on the other hand, I liked it when men I dated opened the car door for me. Was I allowed to want both?* [3]

On the other hand, Sabrina Schaeffer, executive director of the Independent Women's Forum, argued that gender roles help both men and women navigate the often rough waters of courtship, marriage and sex; that ignoring such roles creates confusion.[4]

---

[1] Martha Rampton, 'The Three Waves of Feminism', *Pacific Magazine*, Fall 2008.

[2] Quoted in Rampton. *Pinkfloor* seems to be the web name of Camilla Lyngbo Hjort.

[3] *How To Expect Chivalry From Men In The Age Of Feminist Thinking*, yourtango.com.

[4] Fourth wave feminism showed how many women have been sexually abused by men, particularly by the famous. Women are called upon not only to open their eyes to sexism but actively shout back at it. It is the shouting that characterises the fourth wave.

Feminism and freemasonry

Feminism has created significant changes in male roles and self-perception. When the Titanic sank, 75% of females survived while 80% of males died, but this world, and the one in which freemasons treat their *Good Ladies* to an annual Ladies' Festival, is a long way from Elizabeth Peters' remark:

> *I disapprove of matrimony as a matter of principle … Why should any independent, intelligent female choose to subject herself to the whims and tyrannies of a husband? I assure you, I have yet to meet a man as sensible as myself!* [1]

And from Ayaan Hirsi Ali's view that:

> *As a woman you are better off in life earning your own money. You couldn't prevent your husband from leaving you or taking another wife, but you could have some of your dignity if you didn't have to beg him for financial support.* [2]

Women have long felt their work/life balance to be out of kilter, but men in 2000 began to think they too were struggling to meet the increased range of demands made of them.

Rejection

The *end of rules* involved a rejection of the old ways and our institution became seen as part of the establishment and, perhaps for the first time, counter-cultural. The flow of younger candidates slowed and the seeds of our decline were sown. Nevertheless, this period was very much about values and showed how men and women will respond to ethical ideals when they can see them clearly. What followed was the destruction of those ideals, even though as Freemasons we should continue to believe with Fidel Castro, that *Un mondo mejor es posible*, a better world is possible. [3]

---

[1] Elizabeth Peters, *Crocodile on the Sandbank*, Grand Central Publishing, 1975.

[2] *Infidel*, Simon & Schuster, 2008.

[3] For freemasonry's connection with Castro, see *Masonic Legends*, David West & Matthew West, Hamilton House, 2018.

Phase two – Show me the money: 1980–2000

Rock historian Sean Egan described the Rolling Stones in 1964 as *representatives of opposition to an old, cruel order – the antidote to a class-bound, authoritarian culture.* Joe Cocker's 1969 Woodstock performance of *With a little help from my friends* was eight minutes of passion, an anthem to brotherly love, but in the same year the Stones' *Gimme Shelter,* on the album *Let it Bleed,* was being described as a song *to symbolize … the death of the decade's utopian spirit.* Mick Jagger called it *a kind of end-of-the-world song, really. It's apocalypse.*[1] The revolution was over. The historian William Chafe noted that even in 1967:

> … *the shrill attacks on 'establishment' values from the left were matched by an equally vociferous defense of traditional values by those who were proud of all their society had achieved. If feminists, blacks, antiwar demonstrators, and advocates for the poor attacked the status quo with uncompromising vehemence, millions of other Americans rallied around the flag and made clear their intent to uphold the lifestyle and values to which they had devoted their lives.*[2]

Bill Clinton said:

> *If you look back on the sixties and think there was more good than bad, you're probably a Democrat. If you think there was more harm than good, you're probably a Republican.*[3]

Reagan and Thatcher

The reaction that Chafe spoke of came to fruition in 1981 when Ronald Reagan became President of the United States, two years after Margaret Thatcher had become the British Prime Minister. The two developed a close relationship and both attempted to reverse the policies of their predecessors, by reducing taxation and government spending. Both accepted *trickle-down*[4], the theory that reduced taxation for the wealthy would produce spending to

---

[1] Quotes from *Rolling Stone* magazine.

[2] Chafe, William H, *The Unfinished Journey: America Since World War II*, Oxford Univ. Press, 2006.

[3] Speaking at *BookExpo America* in Chicago, June 3, 2004.

[4] As H.W. Arndt said, *Trickle-down is a myth which should be exposed and laid to rest.* 'The Trickle-Down Myth', *Economic Development and Cultural Change*, October 1983.

provide jobs for the poor. Thatcher said that her policies were:

... based not on some economics theory, but on things I and millions like me were brought up with: an honest day's work for an honest day's pay; live within your means; put by a nest egg for a rainy day; pay your bills on time; support the police. [1]

That is not how the rich become rich, nor are home economics similar to government economics. Nevertheless, what she said was an earnest of her and Reagan's intentions. [2] Thatcher sought to reduce the costs of social services, education and housing, and Reagan saw economic dangers even in health programmes:

One of the traditional methods of imposing statism or socialism on a people has been by way of medicine. It's very easy to disguise a medical program as a humanitarian project . . . Now, the American people, if you put it to them about socialized medicine and gave them a chance to choose, would unhesitatingly vote against it. We have an example of this. Under the Truman administration it was proposed that we have a compulsory health insurance program for all people in the United States, and, of course, the American people unhesitatingly rejected this. [3]

Thatcher-ism

Of course, Thatcherism was a response not only to the philosophical changes of the 1960s but also to the damaging inflation of the 1970s. Beginning with Edward Heath's Conservative government in 1970, inflation peaked at 25% in 1976. It was put down to decimalisation, a sudden rise in oil prices, a

---

[1] Quoted in the *News of the World*, September 1981.
[2] Reagan cut income taxes but he also tripled the Federal debt.
[3] Radio address on *Socialized Medicine*, 1961.

wage/price spiral caused by over-powerful trades union or a loose monetary policy.[1] As a reaction to this experience of inflation both UK and US governments adopted an overtight tight monetary and fiscal policy which caused the recession from 1979 to 1981. Unemployment in the UK rose steeply but, unlike Macmillan's one-nation toryism, Thatcher accepted unemployment as part of her armoury against the trades union. As Fryer and Stambe write, unemployment is useful because it:

> … *provides a pool of potential workers unable to be unwilling to do the most boring, dirty, dead end, menial, underpaid, temporary, insecure, stressful jobs* [and] *provides competition for jobs from desperate jobseekers allowing employers to drive down wages and working conditions.*[2]

Paul Mason argues that the real aim of the neoliberalism of Thatcher and Reagan (and Pinochet) was the destruction of the unions.

> *Its guiding principle is not free markets, nor fiscal discipline, nor sound money, nor privatization and offshoring − not even globalization. All these were by-products or weapons of its main endeavour: to remove organized labour from the equation.*[3]

The result of Thatcher's actions was to make the rich richer and the poor poorer. She reduced tax rates for high earners to provide greater incentives, as she saw it, but reduced the ability of the trades union to act as a counterbalance. She sold off publicly owned enterprises[4] to reduce the role of the state, creating private as opposed to public monopolies, and reduced controls on the finance industry leading to the banking crash of 2007/8.

---

[1] A commonly accepted explanation is that the culprit was the inability to measure spare capacity in the economy. The Taylor Rule holds that central banks should raise interest rates when (a) inflation is above target or (b) demand exceeds capacity, and vice versa. Successive governments had been unable to see that growth in capacity had slowed, again due to the lack of investment in productivity. Governments drew the incorrect conclusion that slow growth indicated a lack of demand and tried to stimulate it by increasing money supply, hence inflation. Paul Mason views 1973 as a phase change in the Kondratieff cycle sparked off in 1971 by Nixon unpegging the dollar from gold. This set off the stock market crash of 1973, itself exacerbated by the Arab-Israeli war and the resultant oil embargo.

[2] 'Neoliberal austerity and unemployment', *The Psychologist*, Vol. 27, No 4, April 2014.

[3] *Post-capitalism: a guide to our future*, Allen Lane, 2015.

[4] Several 'privatised' companies were owned and run by foreign governments.

She wrote of her admiration for Michael Novak, best known for his book *The Spirit of Democratic Capitalism*,[1] noting that:

> *… what he called 'democratic capitalism' was a moral and social, not just an economic system, that it encouraged a range of virtues and that it depended upon co-operation.*

However, far from encouraging virtues, Thatcher's actions made greed good. Ivan Boesky, speaking at University of California, Berkeley in 1986, said:

> *Greed is all right, by the way. I want you to know that. I think greed is healthy. You can be greedy and still feel good about yourself.* [2]

In the same year, Sir Robert Armstrong, then cabinet secretary, voiced concerns about the 'loadsamoney' culture developing in the City of London. He spoke of the *increasing disquiet among those who dealt with the City*, not just over the levels of remuneration but the corners being cut and money being made in ways bordering on the unscrupulous.[3] Nevertheless, Thatcher praised money, saying: *Nobody would remember the Good Samaritan if he had only good intentions. He had money as well.*[4] In her famous *Sermon on the Mound*,[5] she said, *We are told we must work and use our talents to create wealth*, and then went on to quote from 2 Thessalonians: *If a man will not work he shall not eat.* However, as Dante wrote with more insight, avarice:

> *O'ercasts the world with mourning, under foot,*
> *Treading the good, and raising bad men up.*[6]

The earlier vision of social democracy and cohesion had passed but the individualism that was part of it had not; the reduction in regulation led to white-collar lawlessness. The ideal became the individual who grew rich and in the following twenty years the income of America's richest increased by 250%, while the remaining ninety-nine percent of Americans saw an

---

[1] Simon & Schuster, 1982.

[2] *Independent*, 5 July 2010. Boesky was imprisoned for insider dealing, fined $100 million and banned from working in the financial sector ever again.

[3] Reported in the *Guardian*, March 1986.

[4] TV Interview for *Weekend World*, January 1980.

[5] Delivered to the Church of Scotland in the Edinburgh Assembly Rooms, address: *The Mound*.

[6] *Inferno*, Canto XIX.

increase of less than one percent.[1] A legacy of Thatcherism were the *me* years. Centred on *my* demands for *what* I want, *when* I want it, Britain became a society prizing money as a badge of success and a route to instant gratification. Those with money spent it extravagantly,[2] and those without it borrowed on credit cards. It should not be necessary to say that brotherly love may be about *us* or even *you*, but it is certainly not about *me*.

The 'undeserving' poor again

Thatcher spoke of what she said was a Victorian notion:

> ... *they distinguished between the 'deserving' and the 'undeserving poor'. Both groups should be given help : but it must be help of very different kinds if public spending is not just going to reinforce the dependency culture. The problem with our welfare state was that ... we had failed to remember that distinction and so we provided the same 'help' to those who had genuinely fallen into difficulties and needed some support till they could get out of them, as to those who had simply lost the will or habit of work and self-improvement.*[3]

The notion of the undeserving poor pre-dates the Victorian era and was used to justify the workhouse, an institution so deliberately unpleasant that only the genuine poor would enter it. You may recall that, despite this, outdoor relief continued. Decency recognised that poverty had always threatened even the most deserving. Nevertheless, Thatcher claimed to have identified a mass of people too lazy to work. This was her greatest legacy: the fictitious claim of a significant group of undeserving poor, a used to justify some of the cruellest actions of any government during the Cameron/May years.

The 2013 *Annual Fraud Indicator*[4] reported that the largest fraud losses were suffered by UK companies at just under £16.0 billion for the year, and 31% of total fraud. Tax fraud came in second at £14 billion, although this official figure is widely regarded as an underestimate.[5]

---

[1] Mason, *op. cit.* The top 1% are those earning more than $341,000 per year in 2008.

[2] In 2002, at the Petrus restaurant in London, six bankers spent more than $62,700 mostly on wine. The owner was so impressed he did not charge for the food. *New York Times*.

[3] Margaret Thatcher, *The Downing Street Years*, HarperCollins, 1993.

[4] National Fraud Office, © Crown Copyright 2013.

[5] Tax Research UK estimated the gap between tax owed and tax collected in 2012 at £120 billion.

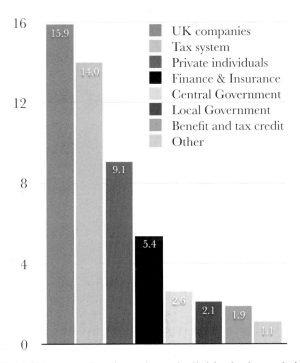

A further £9.1 billion was lost by private individuals through identity theft, mass marketing and online ticket frauds. Finance and insurance scams, including credit card, online banking and cheque fraud amounted to nearly $6 million. Benefits and tax credit fraud amounted to just over one percent of total fraud, coincidentally the same cost as errors made by the Department of Work and Pensions. Put this one percent into perspective. UK supermarkets keep a close eye on what is called *shrinkage*, theft in one form or another from their stores. In 2012-13, this amounted to 1.3% of sales.[1] Of course, the supermarkets try to reduce this, but not at the cost of infuriating the great majority of their customers who are honest. It is no more true to say that benefits claimants are scroungers than it is to say that shoppers at Waitrose or Aldi are dishonest.

In fact people do not claim their due. Unclaimed benefit in 2014 was just over £7.5 billion, just about four times as much as fraud. If you wanted to ensure that people took all and only what they were due, and meant it, you

[1] *Retail Crime in the UK*, Centre for Retail Research.

would be £5.6 billion out of pocket. The political use of the words *scroungers* and *workshy* echo the nineteenth century complaints about the *dishonest poor*, and the choice of all these words is designed to excuse a lack of compassion. If I can prove to myself that you are undeserving, I don't have to bother with you. *Scrounger* is a nasty, divisive and dishonest word.

A homeless man died just outside the House of Commons in February 2018.

If the undeserving poor exist, they form a very small percentage of the population. Much more important than any *dishonest poor* are the undeserving rich. Richard Murphy[1] writes that if Italy, Greece and Spain had taken tax evasion seriously, there would have been no euro crisis. The gap between legally avoided tax and morally due tax is beyond belief. Democrat nomination contender, Bernie Sanders wrote:[2]

> *In 2015 alone, American corporations held a total of $2.4 trillion in offshore profits in tax haven countries, deferring payment of some $700 billion in US taxes.*

---

[1] 'Collect the evaded tax, avoid the cuts,' *Guardian* 25 November 2011

[2] *Our Revolution*, Profile Books, 2016.

The *Sunday Times* reported that

> *Six of Britain's 10 biggest multinationals — including Shell, British American Tobacco (BAT) and Lloyds Banking Group — paid no UK corporation tax in 2014 despite combined global profits of more than £30bn.*[1]

The chair of the UK Public Accounts Committee, Dame Margaret Hodge, said that the tax paid by multinational firms with large UK operations was:

> *... outrageous and an insult to British businesses and individuals who pay their fair share. The inescapable conclusion is that multinationals are using structures and exploiting current tax legislation to move offshore profits that are clearly generated from economic activity in the UK.*[2]

Two UK Parliamentary Select committees gave as their opinion that the company Carillion collapsed as a result of the *recklessness, hubris and greed* of its directors. Carillion managed construction projects and government services ranging from school meals to prison maintenance as well as NHS cleaning, and went into insolvency in January 2018. More than 2,000 people were made redundant. The committees said that the directors sought to increase dividends to protect their own bonuses. The directors left the pension scheme underfunded because they said *it was a waste of money*. 27,000 current and former employees received reduced pensions as a result. The Parliamentary Select committees found the accountants KPMG complicit in signing off Carillion's increasingly fantastical figures, and the internal auditor Deloitte for failing to identify risks in the financial controls, or of being too ready to ignore them.

Reports from the *Guardian*, May 2018

---

[1] 31 Jan 2016.
[2] *BBC News*, 3 December 2016.

Reflections on the first two phases

The hundred years of the middle class period was a long time, even for freemasonry, and we became so accustomed to a constant flow of candidates that the modern problem grew, almost unseen, for another half century.

Denial

Even as candidates became rare, lodges were blithely confident that they would return; that membership was a cyclical matter; that they just needed a few younger brethren; that it was really a matter of too many new lodges being formed ... and so on. Whatever the excuse, we were sure that any membership decline was temporary. Henderson and Belton point to New Zealand where the *'Condition of the Craft' Committee, against a background of a 25% fall in membership between 1963 and 1982, was forecasting a further decrease of 30% by 2001.* The view from the top was that all was well. Busfield reports leaders as saying:

> *1981 – I can assert that there is growing evidence to show that we have arrested the decline ... the future now offers real hope of improvement.*
>
> *1982 – The decline is showing signs of leveling off and we will, I am confident, show an increase in the near future.*
>
> *1983 – With the co-operation and support of all members there will be an early return to increasing membership.*
>
> *1984 – We have inherited a wonderful institution which I believe is in a healthy condition.*[1]

It is unfair to single out one Grand Lodge. Such statements were common during our decline. A member of the UGLE Membership Focus Group said that *we're getting lots of people wanting to join*[2] as late as 2014, while certificates issued at Freemasons' Hall had declined by 6% from the previous year.[3] We really must avoid complacency. The problem won't go away on its own. Until

---

[1] Busfield, Alan, 'The Last Forty Years of Freemasonry', *Proceedings of the United Masters Lodge No. 167,* Auckland, New Zealand, Vol. 26, 1986.

[2] 'Open Forum', in *Freemasonry Today,* Autumn 2014.

[3] *Report of the Board of General Purposes,* December 2017.

we understand that it is systemic, we cannot begin to solve it. As Will Murray puts it … *the ability to believe exactly what you want to believe to be true, even though you are miles off, is the last refuge of those in denial.* [1]

End of predictability

Victorian values included service and the satisfaction of doing a good job. Gunn and Bell instance a surgeon who, retiring in 2000, talked about *vocation, dedication and a duty of care.* They contrast this with the words of his son, an accountant:

> *If I'm brutally honest about why I'm at work I wouldn't say it's for pleasure. I'm trying to earn money to guarantee a sense of security for myself and for my family. Money is what drives me to be at work.*

What certainly had gone away was the middle class ideal of a career:

> *… the middle class notion of the career was a compact between the organisation and individual. The middle class employee promised loyalty to the organisation, personal probity, hard work and deference to the hierarchical order. In return, the organisation repaid this commitment by assuring job security, a salary that would increase progressively with age and the opportunity of promotion over time …* [2]

Richard Scase commented:

> *In the 1970s middle class privileges are undermined in a fundamental way for the first time. The major factor that undermines them is the end of job security, jobs for life. Suddenly because organisations are restructuring and using computer technology in their management systems, managers find they are prone to redundancy … From the 1970s onwards middle classes in Britain are never the same again.* [3]

In *Funky Business*, Ridderstråle and Nordstrom[4] argue that the predictability of jobs and work has gone. People today cannot expect to find a safe job in a safe company, work their way up the hierarchy and comfortably retire forty or so years later. We have to accept that brethren can no longer make a

---

[1] Will Murray, *Corporate Denial*, Capstone Publishing, 2004.

[2] Gunn & Bell, *op.cit.*

[3] Richard Scase & Robert Goffee, *Reluctant Managers*, Routledge, 1989.

[4] Pearson Education, 2000.

commitment to attend every meeting of the lodge of instruction, or even every lodge meeting. They will no doubt do their best but if we think the less of them for their absences, we will lose them.

Freemasonry has had difficulties with retention as well as recruitment, hence the introduction of the mentoring scheme.1 Lodges have not been doing a very good job in looking after their new members, primarily because they have not recognised the different drummers that people have to march to. Members of one lodge that I spoke to, complained that of the last six candidates they had initiated, five had left. To lose one initiate may be regarded as a misfortune, to lose five looks like carelessness, and the oft-heard Past Master's remark, *When I was initiated …* has almost no relevance today.

Change in the source of candidates

The average age of our members is increasing, and the men they meet are also ageing. As we age, we meet fewer new people and our social circle tightens. In all probability, if existing friends and family have ever indicated an interest in freemasonry, they would have already been invited. As a source of candidates, our existing members are a declining force.

The questions we ask candidates and our leadership's recommendations on recruitment still assume that candidates are friends or family of existing members. We properly stress the importance of vetting a candidate's suitability but place the primary responsibility for this on the proposer and seconder, implying that the candidate has one of each before being considered by the lodge. This is increasingly unlikely. 80% of candidates in my mother lodge come via its website.[2]

The questions we ask make assumptions about a society which has largely ceased to exist. For example, some lodges still ask the question, *Would your wife or partner be supportive of our social functions?* Today a wife or partner is very likely to have her own career and interests. While no doubt happy to attend when

---

[1] With what one must admit is patchy success. The lodge Mentor must work hand in glove with the Secretary and Almoner and be in constant touch with all brethren.

2 St Laurence Lodge No. 5511 initiates four or five candidates a year. See *Things to do when you have nothing to do - never be short of candidates again*, David West, Hamilton House, 2014.

her diary allows, she would not see her husband's or partner's interests as in any way binding upon her. Some lodges still tell candidates that *Freemasonry is not a form of life assurance* and ask, *Have you made provision for your family?* with the implication that the man is the breadwinner and takes responsibility for the finances of his wife/partner and family. We really must recognise that a candidate's wife or partner really isn't waiting at home, oven gloves in hand and the table laid, for when he returns from work.

The old man in the sky

We ask, *Do you believe in the existence of a supreme being?* Freemasonry deemed regular by UGLE demands that all candidates express such a belief,[1] but almost all candidates have to be coached to answer in the affirmative, even when they may feel uncomfortable in doing so.

The consolation of religion is less sought today than ever before. Callum Brown's description of the church's experience is uncannily similar to ours:

> *The 1950s was in fact a deeply old-fashioned era ... Nearly 2 million people came to hear Billy Graham preach in London ... in 1954, and a further 1.2 million came in Glasgow in 1955, with 100,000 worshippers packing Hampden Park football stadium for a single religious service.*[2]

By 1983 about a third of the UK population had no religion and by 2011 that third had become a half.[3] The decline has been most marked in those aged 18 to 24 – by 2014, 64% had no religion.

> *Britain is becoming less religious, with the numbers who affiliate with a religion or attend religious services experiencing a long-term decline. And this trend seems set to continue; not only as older, more religious generations are replaced by younger, less*

---

[1] The phrase, *and his revealed will,* seems to have dropped out of fashion.

[2] *The Death of Christian Britain,* Routledge, 2001, 2nd edition 2009.

[3] The wording of the question affects the outcome. In a 2012 YouGov survey 76% claimed they were not very religious or not religious at all. The 2008 European Social Survey asked *Which religion or denomination do you belong to at present?* 52.68% said none. The 2009 British Social Attitudes survey asked *Do you regard yourself as belonging to any particular religion?* 50.67% said no. The 2010 Labour Force Survey asked *What is your religion even if you are not currently practising?* 22.4% said none. The 2011 census asked *What is your religion?* 25.1% said none.

religious ones, but also as the younger generations increasingly opt not to bring up their children in a religion.[1]

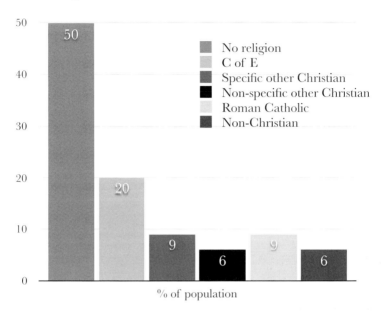

% of population

In 1970s Ireland, more than 90% of the population attended mass on a Sunday, but by 2013, following the paedophile scandals, attendance had fallen to 34%, and by 2018, to 18%. Many people in Ireland describe themselves as *post-Catholics;* the *Irish Catholic* calls them *functionally atheist.*[2]

> *It took several centuries … to convert Britain to Christianity, but it has taken less than forty years for the country to forsake it … Quite suddenly in 1963, something very profound ruptured the character of the nation and its people, sending organised Christianity on a downward spiral to the margins of social significance.*[3]

More recent figures continue this trend. An analysis of the 2017 British Social Attitudes survey indicated that among young people *almost three out of four 18 to 24 year olds say they have no religion, a rise of nine percentage points since 2015* and *53% of all adults describe themselves as having no religious affiliation.* The chart on baptismal rates that we saw earlier showed a slight increase in

[1] *British Social Attitudes*, 2011–2012.

[2] Michael Kelly, editor of the *Irish Catholic* newspaper, 2012.

[3] Callum Brown, *op. cit.*

religiosity from 1900 to 1930, but from 1950 to 2000 there was rapid decline, a period described as *the slow death of Christian Britain*.[1]

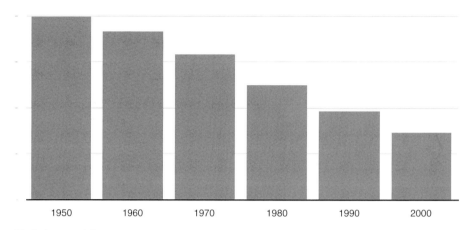

Religion and freemasonry

The whole question of religious belief, if this is not too bad a pun, is up in the air. No theologian accepts the *old man in the sky;* 16% of practising C of E clergy do not accept a personal god.[2] Many religions reject such a concept. The *great spirit* in indigenous North American beliefs:

> ... *probably existed in the ancient beliefs of some tribes, but is generally inconsistent with the spirit of egalitarianism and democracy that characterises most tribal groups.*[3]

Paul Tillich, one of the greatest of modern theologians, viewed god not as *a being* but as *being itself*, the ground of existence, and to demand of a candidate that he have a belief in *the old man in the sky* would prevent the initiation not only of atheists but also of theologians – and of Native Americans.

I am not arguing for the removal of the VSL or prayers from lodge. I would, however, argue that the question on religious belief might be modified such that it reads more like the question on monarchy. On the pattern of *Are you happy to drink the health of Her Majesty?* we might ask, *Are you happy to participate in prayers in lodge?*

---

[1] Callum Brown, *op. cit.*

[2] *Yougov* survey of clergy in 2014.

[3] David M. Jones & Brian L. Molyneaux, *Mythology of the American Nations*, Hermes House, 2009.

An American view

Having reviewed a draft of this book, Kirk C. White, author of *Operative Freemasonry: a manual for restoring light and vitality to the fraternity*, kindly observed:

> The preceding chapter makes reference to the young men who identify as 'none' on recent surveys of religious affiliation. As Dr West correctly points out, this is a growing demographic right in the middle of freemasonry's recruitment pool and we would do well to find ways to include them. However, we should not be too ready to conflate them with atheists, especially in America.
>
> The general consensus within the American Academy of Religions is that such 'nones' are more likely to be spiritual seekers who have rejected affiliation with organized denominations and what they see as undesirably prescriptive, one-size-fits-all, ethical codes. Such men seek a close connection to divinity but don't want to be told what that divinity looks like, nor how it should be worshipped. They seek the doors to spiritual experience but wish to open those doors themselves and gain their own, unmediated experience, from which they can build their own moral code.
>
> Such men are religiously unaffiliated but they are not atheists. Many of them are the same men who are drawn to non-traditional, non-prescriptive religions such as those of the modern paganisms (Wicca, Druidry, etc.), and here in the USA a significant percentage of new masons are modern pagans. There are entire lodges of men who identify as pagan; enough that a past Grand Master of Florida tried to have them banned from membership in our fraternity; an attempt that was rightfully rejected as a violation of our landmarks.
>
> To my mind, freemasonry has much to offer such men. We do not tell them who or how to worship (although here in the US, many Grand Lodges still insist on monotheism) but rather give them the opportunity, resources and support to find the divine in their own way, helping them towards a dialogue about how to translate those experiences into personal moral and ethical codes for daily life.

Phase 3 – The end of decency: 2000–present

Thatcher's rejection of anything resembling socialism was also a rejection of the idealism. As Beth Butler, a teacher aged 79, said:

> *What did we lose? A zest; a get-up-and-go; an optimism. People seemed to become gradually more passive under Thatcher, as though the colour had gone out of their lives. Possessions suddenly became far more important, too. Fashion, clothes and shoes – and the concomitant rise in fake goods. It was as though the zest for life had been replaced by self-centredness. People were interested in what they had for themselves, rather than doing things together.* [1]

Freemasonry has values far beyond self-interest, as the Royal Arch lectures on the *Robes and Sceptres* tell us. The first lecture could well emanate from the human relations movement in management:

> *Your sceptre bears a crown … Let it, however, remind you that to reign sovereign in the hearts and affections of men is far more gratifying to a generous and benevolent mind than to rule over their lives and fortunes …*

The second lecture talks of *union* and *harmony*, and of the *all-seeing eye* borne by the Second Principal's sceptre that instructs him *to stand as a watchman on a tower, to admonish the companions to fidelity and industry;* words that might have come straight from Dr Heaton, or indeed Samuel Smiles. The third speaks of *universal beneficence and charity* and the mitre on the Third Principal's sceptre is *an emblem of dignity,* but there is no dignity in *Greed is all right, by the way. I want you to know that.* An objective for the renaissance of freemasonry must be to restore such dignity.

> *Let me impress upon your minds, and may it be instilled into your hearts, that every human creature has a just claim on your kind offices. I therefore trust that you will be good to all. More particularly do I recommend to your care the household of the faithful, that diligence and fidelity in the duties of your respective vocations, liberal beneficence and diffusive charity, by constancy and sincerity in your friendships … [may] prove to the world the happy and beneficial effects of our ancient and honourable institution.* [2]

---

[1] *The Guardian*, 13 April 2013

[2] *The Long Closing* in *St Laurence Working* (ed. David West), St Laurence Lodge, No. 5511, 2010.

Nasty, grovelling and greedy

When the novelist Simon Raven died in 2001, Charles Spencer wrote of his:

> ... *most cherished themes and obsessions – chiefly sex, betrayal, decay and death, as well as the possibility of maintaining some degree of honour in a fallen world.* [1]

In many ways Raven's views on behaviour echo those of Cardinal Newman. He wrote that up to the 1960s Englishmen held fast to the rule that *they should not irritate, nag, scold, embarrass or in any way incommode* other people, that they should *never interfere, pry or delate,* a wonderful Raven phrase, but in 1985 he described a generation that had become *shrill, demanding and hysterical, self pitying and unctuous; full of grievance at their own lot and envy of others' attainments.* [2]

Simon Raven was famously described as having *the mind of a cad but the pen of an angel,* but he took a moral, if caustic, view of the world despite, or because of, creating some of the most scurrilous characters in literature. Mrs Holbrook in *The Rich Pay Late* is an academic who explains why she does not leave her dreadful husband:

> '*I should miss him. You see ... he personifies the folly and meanness of the human race. Since I tend to live on a rather remote level of my own, it is salutary to be daily reminded of the sort of man by whom and for whom the world is mostly run. If I am ever in danger of thinking the truth lies there'* – she indicated the books around them – '*I can always take a look at your father. Nasty, grovelling, greedy – he is the truth about the world, Jude, and it does not do to forget it.*' [3]

Raven might have been amused, but more likely outraged, that his Mr Holbrook would become a quite normal figure in the years that followed his death. Mr Holbrook perfectly symbolises phase three of our account of social change since the 1950s.

This phase has been bad enough to create the possibility of our resurgence. Many men find this society distasteful and are looking elsewhere for meaning and values. We can offer them a moral haven.

[1] Charles Spencer, 'Dangerously, deliciously addictive', *Daily Telegraph*, 19 May 2001.

[2] *Alms for Oblivion*, Simon Raven, Vol II, Vintage, 2012.

[3] *Alms for Oblivion*, Simon Raven, Vol I, Vintage, 2012.

Reversal in management theory

A new theory of business occurred in about 2000. It was quite contrary to the logical processes laid of Taylor and Fayol, and equally contrary to the psychology of the OD movement. This new theory held that it was the CEO alone who created all value in a company, and companies set off in a search for the one magical person who would give all direction, make all decisions and create all innovations. It is as if all the research undertaken on management since the 1930s never took place. Even Fayol, with his top down processes, did not believe in magicians.

A series of Mary Poppins-like figures came forward. Few succeeded. Most failed quite horribly but this has not reversed the philosophy, despite the predictable results of system glitches and customer dissatisfaction. In 2014, banking leaders suggested *that their organisations are too vast and their activities too convoluted and technical for them to understand.*[1] The implications of such a remark are too painfully obvious to bear stating here.

The decline of employee engagement and morale

> University of Pennsylvania research found that capital improvements increase productivity by 3.9%. Investing in engagement and loyalty increases it by 8.5%.

One result of this was a rapid decline in employee engagement in almost all companies as the aim of management changed from long-term success fuelled by interpersonal trust and creativity, to short-term profit and earnings per share, through cost reduction, downsizing and plain cheating. Work lost much of its meaning and job satisfaction reached an all-time low. Those who have studied management will not be surprised that companies who remained true to earlier ideals proved to be far more successful than those who single-mindedly sought profit.[2]

A 2008 Gallup survey found that only 13% of German employees were engaged with their workplace, and fully one-fifth of the workforce, was

---

[1] *Independent*, 17 November 2014.

[2] Prime examples being John Lewis, Lincoln Electric, Southwest Airlines, the steel company Nucor, Iceland (voted best company to work for in 2012 and 2014) and the Brazilian firm Semco which grew its revenues from US$4 million in 1982 to US$212 million by 2003.

actively disengaged. This is an astounding result for a society like Germany.[1] The UK Chartered Management Institute reported that only one-third of UK employees trusted their management, a figure which represented an all-time low.[2] The results of the 2009 Ipsos Loyalty Study indicated that only a quarter of US employees thought their company deserved their loyalty.

In 2004, UK research indicated that managers were working nearly 10% more hours than in 1984 and that stress was causing a loss of 13 million working days a year.[3] By 2017, the average working week had increased in most parts of the UK. Many of our brethren are in teaching and a 2018 National Education Union Survey showed that four out of five teachers in England considered leaving the profession because of their workload. To meet the demands of the job, they had to work twenty or more additional hours each week at home. Contrary to the Human Relations movement of the 1960s and 70s, they also suffered micro-management:

> *We are not trusted to get on and do our job. We are accountable at every level, which creates more stress and paperwork.*[4]

In 2018, majority of people were just going to work, not enjoying it nor finding satisfaction in a job well done. Many people, many of them our members, will have been tired, not exhilarated, at the end of the day – which has obvious implications for the lodge of instruction. Worse,

> *… the percentage of employees who experienced some form of retaliation for blowing the whistle was 22 percent, an all-time high. This compares with 15 percent in 2009 and 12 percent in 2007. The proportion of respondents who felt they couldn't question management without fear of retaliation amounted to 19 percent of all employees.*[5]

---

[1] Marco Nink, 'Employee Disengagement Plagues Germany', *Business Journal*, April 2009. Similar results were obtained in the USA: 29% engaged, 17% actively disengaged.

[2] Kerstin Alfes et al., *Creating an engaged workforce; findings from the Kingston employee engagement consortium project*, CIPD 2010.

[3] Will Murray, *op. cit.*

[4] *I don't know how I can change how I work, I don't know how long I can maintain it, and the impact that it's having on my family is horrific*, one teacher said.

[5] Curtis C. Verschoor, 'New Survey of Workplace Ethics Shows Surprising Results', *Accounting WEB*, April 2012.

The Fraud Advisory Panel issued a report entitled *Business Behaving Badly* in 2017. The results made unpleasant reading. A good percentage of corporate frauds were inside jobs and there was an increase in frauds committed by senior management. A majority of employees believe that their senior management would act unethically to improve their company's results and at least a quarter of UK employees see bribery and corruption as widespread. Serious ethical breaches are committed by people who think that is their job.

Managerialism

Early capitalism featured a capitalist risking his own money in a venture. That capitalist took a day-to-day interest in the affairs of the company and any business loss or fine for a misdemeanour affected him or her personally. Companies are now run by managers. It is rare for them to suffer for losses or misdemeanours. Failures affect only the share price, often in odd ways.

> BP shares rose after a US judge capped the maximum fine it faced for the Gulf of Mexico disaster at £9 billion ($13.7 billion), ruling that BP had released 3.2 million barrels of oil into the sea. The US government had estimated 4.2 million. The fine was the largest ever levied in the US for pollution. BP announced a £12 billion ($18.7 billion) deal to settle all outstanding claims in the US. BP closed up 3.67%. The total cost to BP was £34.4 billion ($53.8 billion). *Independent* 2015.

Under managerialism, morality is not a criterion for business decision-making, a common view being that the only proper aim for management is profit maximisation. The question for management is not what is the right thing to do, but what incurs the least cost.

Loyalty is a two way street but with managerialism rewards are all one way. Sean O'Grady reported in 2014 that despite a ten year decline in share prices, the remuneration of senior managers had quadrupled since 2000.[1] Smith and Kuntz, writing for *Bloomberg*, reported that while in the 1950s the average US CEO received 20 times as much as the average worker in his or her company, by 2013 the multiple in the US had reached 204.[2] Ronald Johnson's pay as CEO of J.C. Penney in 2012 was an amazing 1,795 times

---

[1] *Independent*, 5 July 2010.
[2] The average multiple in UK blue chip companies reached 130 in 2015, measured against their own company workers, but 183 against average pay of all workers.

that of the average J.C. Penney worker. He was CEO for 18 months and left after a 25% drop in sales.[1] In 2016 Thomas Rutledge of Charter Communications Inc. received a pay increase of 499% and was paid $98 million. In 2018, The Motley Fool said:

> *Charter doesn't really have a major pillar of growth it can lean on, and it disappointed speculators by rejecting a buyout offer from Verizon last year. Charter doesn't pay a dividend - as Verizon, AT&T, and Comcast all do - and its stock isn't cheap at 67 times next year's earnings. This all makes Charter a tough stock to get excited about.*

The usual leader in UK CEO pay, Sir Martin Sorrell, saw his package drop from £70.4 million to £48.1 million. He resigned in April 2018 *ahead of the findings of an investigation into alleged personal misconduct* as the *Guardian* put it. The CIPD reported that:

> *Carnival was ordered to pay £32 million in penalty charges relating to its deliberate pollution of the seas and intentional acts to cover it up ... the largest-ever criminal penalty involving deliberate vessel pollution.*[2]

In the same year, the remuneration for its CEO, Arnold Donald, increased from £6 million to £22 million. Note the words *deliberate*, *intentional* and *criminal*. As the director of Corporate Governance and Pension Investment for the American Federation of State, County and Municipal Employees, Richard Ferlauto, said, *What does 'pay for performance' mean if you ignore performance?*

UK banks and building societies have received a total of 19.7 million complaints, (almost 9,000 a day) since the middle of 2008. A spokesman for the Robin Hood Tax campaign, said: *Far from banks clearing up their act after causing the crisis, they've continued to treat the public they should be serving with contempt.*The Financial Conduct Authority reported that financial firms were the subject of in 3.32 million complaints in the first half of 2017, compared with 3.04 million in the second half of 2016. Total redress paid to consumers in the first half of 2017 was £1.99 billion.

Management credibility is at risk. How can a senior executive understand the needs, fears, abilities and motivations of people when his/her life is so utterly and radically different from theirs? The reward for CEOs is so often at the

---

[1] Elliot Blair Smith and Phil Kuntz, *Bloomberg*, April 30 2013

[2] *Executive Pay*, Chartered Institute of Personnel & Development, 2017.

expense of the employees. Pay freezes, reductions in sickness benefits, and non-payment of bonuses lead to a reduction in costs for the company, which in turn leads to increased profitability, and thus greater reward for the CEO. The CEO of the International Airlines Group (IAG) was paid £6.4m in 2014, an increase of 30% on the previous year after IAG had reported after-tax profits of more than £730m. The company said the results were achieved by making 4,500 people redundant (about a quarter of the workforce) and reducing employment terms and conditions for crew at the airline Iberia.[1] The boss is the enemy

All in this together?

I visited the Falklands in 2016 and was struck by a contrast:

Memorial in Stanley, Falkland Islands

British soldiers were issued with the same rations regardless of rank; however the Argentinean officers had different rations to their men. The officers' ration pack was twice the size of the other ranks'. It also contained items such as writing paper and a miniature of whisky. This made them highly prized by British troops.[2]

Did this have anything to do with the result? It is hard to think that it didn't.

Without fanfare, the Company Commander, sited between 4 and 5 Platoons said, 'OK, let's go!' and stepped over the embankment. Swallowing hard, I croaked something similar and also climbed out to commence our advance. I took only a few paces and glanced to my left. From my position as right hand assault platoon commander, I could see the OC (very closely followed by his signaller), the 4 Platoon Commander and, barely in the gloom, the right hand assault platoon commander of A Company. And no-one else. For what

---

[1] The CEO declined a 2% increase in his basic pay for 2015 amounting to £17,000. The IAG annual report said: *Once again, the chief executive has continued to lead by example in proposing restraint in executive packages!*

[2] Royal Marines Museum.

must have been only the briefest of moments, but which seemed a lifetime, it appeared the officers and one signaller alone were advancing on the enemy. Then, with a muttering of barely audible curses, the men of A and B Companies spilled forward to assault Wireless Ridge. [1]

Brotherly love may be defined in part by the phrase *all in it together.*

Following an inadequate meal of pemmican and pony meat on the night of January, 31, 1909, Shackleton … privately forced upon [Frank Wild] *one of his biscuits from the four that he, like others, was rationed daily. 'I do not suppose that anyone else in the world can … realise how much generosity … was shown by this,' Wild wrote, 'I DO by GOD. I shall never forget it.' … The mystique that Shackleton acquired as a leader may partly be attributed to the fact that he elicited from his men strength and endurance they never imagined they possessed; he ennobled them.* [2]

Poverty and employment

While largesse was being provided to CEOs, the Trussell Trust reported that between 1st April 2016 and 31st March 2017, their foodbanks provided 1.2 million three day emergency food supplies to people in crisis. Of this number, nearly 450,000 went to children. In 45% of cases, the need for emergency food was caused by changes to benefits and delays in payment, but in more than a quarter of cases the cause was low pay. In 2018, National Health Service employees formed the largest proportion of such cases.

The Joseph Rowntree Foundation reported in 2014 that there were as many working families in poverty as non-working ones and two-thirds of people who gained work in 2014 were paid less than the living wage.[3] In 2017, a KPMG report showed that one in five jobs and some five and a half million full-time employees were paid less than the official living wage. The Fraud Advisory Panel said:

Each year the government spends some £27bn supporting the incomes of working people whose jobs don't pay enough to make ends meet.

---

[1] *A Platoon Commander's Perspective*, The Army at army.mod.uk

[2] Caroline Alexander, *The Endurance*, Bloomsbury, 1998.

[3] Tom McInnes *et al.*, *Monitoring Poverty and Social Exclusion 2014*, Joseph Rowntree Foundation. When this was increased to £7.83 per hour in March 2018, the Living Wage Foundation calculated that it was 10.5% less than the amount needed to cover living costs. In London, the new amount was 30% less than needed.

It is perhaps no surprise that in 2017 the demand for *unsecured credit*, mainly payday loans, rose at the fastest pace since the banking fiasco. The Office for National Statistics revealed that the rise in employment from 2008 to end 2013 was not about jobs but about self-employment.

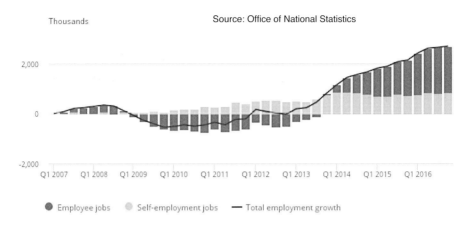

Thousands   Source: Office of National Statistics

● Employee jobs   ● Self-employment jobs   — Total employment growth

Only in 2014 did the number of jobs begin to rise. By November 2017, self-employment represented a higher percentage of employment than at any time in the previous 40 years, and the average income from self-employment had fallen by 22% since 2008. This was not the re-birth of a nation of shopkeepers and entrepreneurs, but companies fiddling the status of their employees to avoid paying National Insurance, holiday and sick pay.

The Bournemouth Daily Echo told a tragic tale:

> *Ruth Lane said she has received no apology or contact from bosses at DPD following husband Don's death last month. Mr Lane, 53, skipped numerous appointments with kidney specialists after he was fined £150 for missing a day's work for attending another hospital visit over his diabetes. His manager told him he could not understand why he required a day off for it and issued a daily fine ... In the space of a year the courier collapsed four times due to his diabetes and missed the appointments as he felt under pressure to cover his rounds. Mr Lane, of Christchurch collapsed at home on December 30 [2018] and died in hospital five days later.*

Partly as a result of this horror story, Robert Booth in reported that:

The courier company DPD is to offer all of its drivers sick pay and paid holidays and will abolish its £150 daily fines for missing work, as part of wholesale reforms to its gig-working model ... [1]

With longer working hours, zero-hour contracts, increased shift work, and worries about the future, many freemasons no longer felt able to take time off to attend a meeting, even when holiday entitlement allowed. In 2018, the UK had become a nasty society, and was forecast to become worse: populist restrictions on flows of labour, and rapid technology advances *will cause the work experience and employee engagement to decline even more.* [2]

Lodges, private and Grand, will have to recognise that the world has changed, no longer suited to the rules appropriate to the years from 1850 to 1950. The situation that we face today is more similar to the society of the early 1800s. Surely we cannot maintain political neutrality in the face of such economic and social changes, if we are to remain true to our values?

---

[1] *The Guardian*, March 2018.
[2] *2017 Trends in Global Employee Engagement*, Aon Hewit.

Reflections on phase 3

When people at work cannot trust management; when their employer extends no loyalty towards them; when they see senior management taking massive rewards (frequently at the expense of their own earnings and job security); when they work longer hours for the same or even less pay; when incompetence is rewarded and dishonesty is endemic at the top; indeed when management become aliens, they are unlikely to invest unthinking trust in any leadership of any kind, our order included.

We will have to demonstrate that our leadership is different; that it does understand the conditions of the ordinary masons who form the bulk of our membership; that it genuinely does seek their opinions and is ready to listen to what they say; that it does not hide itself away in free executive bars; that it pays for its own dining; that it is not a mutually congratulatory clique isolated from reality, and all in all that it genuinely deserves the salutes and ovations it demands. We must demonstrate that in all our actions, we place equality and morality first and reject the sins of arrogance, pride and self-aggrandisement.

I believe that freemasonry can play a major part in the rescue of society and in doing so rescue itself, but we can only do this from a position of moral security. Talk is not enough; the talk has to be walked.

> *Duty, honour, and gratitude now bind you to be faithful to every trust; to support with becoming dignity your new character and to enforce, by example and precept, the tenets of the system. Therefore let no motive cause you to swerve from your duty, violate your vows, or betray your trust; but be true and faithful, and imitate the example of that celebrated artist whom you have once represented. By this exemplary conduct, you will convince the world that merit has been your title to our privileges and that on you our favours have not been undeservedly bestowed.*[1]

The new audience

The middle class from which we recruited from 1850 to 1950 was largely defined by the nature of its employment. Generally speaking, we recruited

---

[1] *St Laurence Working.*

white collar workers with careers in the professions, medium-sized firms, local government and the civil service with an admixture of the self-employed, commonly in building trades. Many members followed their fathers and grandfathers into freemasonry. Many had careers and pensions and valued security and conformity. The new audience is different. Unlikely to be introduced by family members, they make a conscious and personal decision to join us.

They have ideals that they believe we will match and are actively seeking fellowship, meaning and purpose. They have researched our order via the web and know a lot more about us than the earlier audience. They tend to be highly educated,[1] younger, more self-confident and flexible with good inter-personal skills. Some have full time jobs but even then, shift and weekend working is common. A greater number have less secure and even temporary employment in the form of part-time, agency or contracting work. Some have several jobs. Some are self-employed.

Such men will form a good proportion of our new audience and we must remember that the new audience's free time is often unpredictable. We have to adapt to them. We must put in greater efforts to make this new audience feel part of our order. In the past, induction was carried out by the initiates' friends and relations. Now we must consciously plan it for each new member. I repeat that the old PMs' saying, *When I was initiated* ... has little or no value.

Social contract

Thomas Hobbes (1588–1679) sought to explain the existence of communal life by the notion of a *social contract*,[2] an agreement between members of society that laws will govern them all for mutual benefit. Each person agrees *not* to do things they might otherwise want to do, in return for other people agreeing likewise. Hobbes argues that without such an agreement, nothing good can be created:

---

[1] The undergraduate population in the UK peaked at 1,928,140 in 2011/12.

[2] Thomas Hobbes, *Leviathan, or The Matter, Forme and Power of a Common Wealth Ecclesiasticall and Civil*, 1651. (Quotations edited.) Locke, Rousseau and Kant also used the term. The contract is not supposed to be an actual event. Society is explained *as if* a contract were made.

If one plant, sow, build or possess a convenient seat, others may be expected to come to dispossess and deprive him, not only of the fruits of his labour, but also his life.

and good things would be impossible:

There is no place for industry because the fruit thereof is uncertain and consequently no culture of the earth; no navigation, no knowledge of the face of the earth; no account of time; no arts; no letters; no society; [but] continual fear and danger of violent death.

Without the social contract, man would live in a state of nature in which, Hobbes' ringing phrase, the life of man is:

Solitary, poor, nasty, brutish, and short.

Hobbes' social contract was to be enforced by a body which he referred to as the *Commonwealth*, its name indicating its purpose: that by acting in common, society increases wealth for everyone. The Commonwealth acts through the rule of law but while the law is necessary, it is not in itself sufficient. Most of our social relationships are governed by the principles of etiquette and decency where the law is often no remedy. While we may be able to sue a delivery service when a wedding dress arrives late, a financial penalty yields no solace to a bride who cannot look her best.

In normal life we have to trust people. Every failure of trust makes social life that bit more difficult, and trust and trustworthiness are in decline.[1] The annual *Edelman Trust Barometer* in January 2107 announced a *Global Implosion of Trust*. People's trust in the media and in business fell to an all time low. Governments were the least trusted institutions in half of the countries surveyed. Most people thought the politico-economic system unfair, offering little hope for the future.[2] The 2018 Barometer reported that the biggest victim has been truth.

Persistent references to fake news linked to headlines around foreign government election manipulation have, unsurprisingly, had a cumulative, deep effect on the public. The

---

[1] Ray Winn, *Running the Red: An Evaluation of Strathclyde Police's Red Light Camera Initiative - Research Findings*, The Scottish Government Publications, 1999.

[2] Fuelling right wing populist movements, increasingly visible from 2016 onwards: the Trump election, the Brexit vote, Matteo Salvini's far right party in Italy, and the relative success of Marine Le Pen in France, Sebastian Kurz in Austria, and Geert Wilders in Holland.

inability to stem the perceived surge in disinformation has proven toxic: 63 percent of the US general population finds it difficult to distinguish between what is real news and what is fake ... The uncertainty of the moment is palpable. The public is fearful, and trust is disturbingly low.

Social Capital

At a different level, the phrase *social capital* refers to the reservoir of inter-personal trust in society. When people are generally prepared to trust each other, a society has a large reservoir of trust, or high social capital. The willingness to trust is largely the result of social interaction.

The title of Robert Putnam's book, *Bowling Alone*, refers to the fact that while the number of tenpin bowlers in the US increased by about 10% between 1980 and 1993, participation in league bowling almost halved. Of course, Putnam's book is not really about bowling but about the decline of community life in general:

... the numbers imply we now have sixteen million fewer participants in public meetings about local affairs, eight million fewer committee members, eight million fewer local organisation leaders and three million fewer men and women organised to work for better government, than ... in the mid 1970s.

Putnam describes the social change in terms of a Yiddish distinction: that people today are less like *machers* and more like *schmoozers*.

Machers are the doers, the involved people. They take the lead in clubs and associations and are found working on community projects, attending local community and political meetings. In masonry, they are the source of lodge and temple management, secretaries or treasurers, charity stewards, the organisers of charity events, golf days and widows' lunches. They are the reliable folk, the good citizens of their community.

Schmoozers have just as active a social life but one less organised and purposeful. Their use of time is spontaneous and flexible, not planned ahead. They spend time with friends, visit relatives and attend events that interest them, but only when time and motivation coincide. They resist commitment and can readily change plans if something else comes along.

A lodge needs *machers*. Only by having a committed and energetic set of officers can a lodge survive and prosper. This is particularly true of the civil servants of the lodge: the Secretary, DC and Treasurer. Once succession to these offices fails, the lodge's fate is sealed. In society as a whole, *machers* have been slowly disappearing as schmoozing increases, and organisations like our own that require regular commitment have suffered as a result. Putnam thinks of the distinction as psychological but it is just as likely to be sociological, a reaction to changes the changes in society that we have discussed. People have been forced to become *schmoozers* in reaction to shift work, zero-hours contracts, sudden changes in work demands and top-down management.

The decline of social capital and the loss of trust are dangerous to our way of life and both have been declining in our society at an alarming rate. Part of our role in society must be in maintaining and increasing social capital, enabling more good men to work together in greater love and unity, a duty for which we are well suited. We create social capital by loving as brethren. As *British Social Attitudes* reported in 2009:

> *Our findings suggest that those who are more organisationally active tend also to be more trusting of others. They also suggest that it is the fact of affiliation rather than type or extent of activity, that is generally the most decisive factor.*

Hopeful signs

The story so far has been one of doom and gloom, and although this has not been pleasant, it is vital that we understand what has been happening in society if we are to respond. We will not survive if we look the other way. Nevertheless, by 2018 there were some small but hopeful signs pointing towards a possible moral re-awakening.

Bernie Sanders, although officially an independent, was the most important Democratic Party figure during and after the 2016 presidential election in the USA. He was still drawing large crowds a year after Trump won. In his book, *Our Revolution: a future to believe in,*[1] he writes of the need to:

---

[1] 2016, Thomas Dunne Books.

- End the rigged economy. *A job has got to lift workers out of poverty, not keep them in it ... companies all over [the USA] make excessive profits by paying their workers substandard wages with the full expectation that the taxpayers ... [will] subsidise them.*

- End the gender pay gap and enable workers to join trades union. He shows that as union membership declines so the share of national income going to the top 10% increases. He seeks to create a full-employment economy, repairing the country's infrastructure.

- Reform the tax system, which in the USA has a *whole slew of [loopholes] that advantage the wealthy, and a billionaire hedge fund manager can pay a lower effective rate of tax than a truck driver, teacher or nurse.* He seeks the end of offshore tax havens, angrily citing the Bank of America which received $1.3 trillion in bailouts after the banking disaster, and then *set up two hundred subsidiaries in the Caymans. Not only did it pay no federal income taxes that year, it received a tax refund for $1.9 billion.*

- Quite contrary to Reagan's beliefs, Sanders argues that *health care is a right, not a privilege. The United States must join the rest of the industrialised world and guarantee healthcare to every man, woman and child.* Seeking reform of the justice system, he says: *We are spending £$80 billion a year to lock up 2.2 million Americans, disproportionately African-Americans, Latinos and Native Americans.*

It is important to stress that Sanders was speaking to an American audience in America, and yet he came very close indeed[1] to becoming a candidate for the presidency, while refusing to take funds from corporate donors. When he raised twenty million dollars from his supporters in January 2016, the average donation was $27. His support came mainly from the under 45s, and even more so from the under 30s. Sanders' support among young people should have given the party leadership (and freemasonry) something to think about. It was his values, style and beliefs which registered with younger voters, a hopeful sign.

Likewise in the UK general election in 2017, Jeremy Corbyn was supported

---

[1] He won the popular vote in 23 states.

by the younger vote[1] In the 18-24 bracket, 60% voted Labour, with a 16% increased turn out. Corbyn was also funded by individual donations.

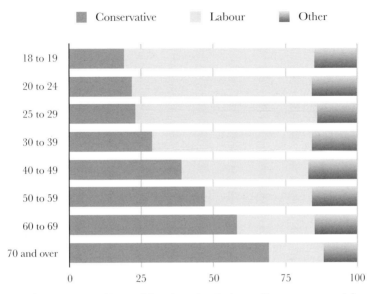

The *Daily Telegraph*, usually no friend to the Labour Party, reported:[2]

> *Jeremy Corbyn's election campaign has been funded by a surge of small donors ... In a marked contrast to the Tory campaign, Labour has received more than 100,000 online donations from members of the public. The drive has raised three million - an average of £22 per donation - since the snap election was called in mid-April.*

In 2010, the Labour Party had 190,000 members. By 2017, membership had climbed to 552,000.[3] The turning point in the 2017 UK election – which was expected to be an overwhelming win for the Conservative Party – came on 10 May 2017, with what was thought to be a dangerous leak of the Labour Party manifesto. The story is wonderfully told by Alex Nunns in his 2018 book, *The Candidate.*[4] Despite all the foreboding, that evening *the Mirror newspaper published a poll revealing that the policies were wildly popular.* The policies

---

[1] Although both were older than their supporters: Sanders born in 1941, Corbyn in 1949.

[2] June 2017

[3] The Conservative Party ceased to report membership in 2013, but in 2017 the Campaign for Conservative Democracy put it at about 70,000.

[4] O/R Books.

had included re-nationalising the railways, the Royal Mail and the energy industry, a strategy which received the support of half the electorate, with only 25% opposed. What is more:

> *Seventy-one per cent wanted zero hours contracts banned. Sixty-three per cent supported the radical idea of requiring any company bidding for public contracts to adopt a maximum pay ratio of 20:1 between their highest and lowest paid staff. Taxing the rich, for so long taboo in British politics, turned out to be a big hit. Sixty five percent liked the idea of raising the income tax of those earning over £80,000, including an absolute majority of Tory voters. And so it continued with policy after policy attracting vast support.*[1]

The evidence showed that in 2017/8 the Conservatives were out of step with other parties: most of their members calling for socially illiberal and authoritarian policies. 84% of Conservatives polled agreed with the statement that schools should teach children to obey authority. They were opposed to gay marriage, supported the death penalty, wanted the return of censorship for films and magazines.

Neither Sanders nor Corbyn won their country's leadership election, although both came very close against all predictions. I am not arguing that all freemasons should vote the Labour or Democrat ticket.[2] My point is that in the face of a society living at the end of decency, it is of some comfort to know that there are a growing number of people, particularly younger ones, who want to move a higher moral ground. It is on these people that our future depends. We must welcome their idealism.

---

[1] Nunns, *op.cit.* It also included such policies as ending tuition fees, lifting the pay block for public sector workers, requiring pay audits to close the gap experienced by women and minorities, scrapping assessments for those with disabilities, and many other radical ideas.

[2] Although an argument can be mounted that neo-liberalism is contrary to masonic beliefs and values. See *stlaurencelodge.org.uk/news/point-within-circle*.

Beyond the present

If freemasonry can get to grips with the end of decency, it still has to face what may well be as big a shift in employment as the industrial revolution itself. Massive uncertainty surrounds artificial intelligence and automation, and numbers vary. The study by Frey and Osbourne[1] indicated that 47% of US workers are in jobs that could be lost to artificial intelligence and automation within the next 10 to 20 years. A similar study for the UK indicated a loss of 30 to 35%.[2]

Such change would not happen over night and PricewaterhouseCoopers (PWC) offer a valuable three phase view of automation.[3]

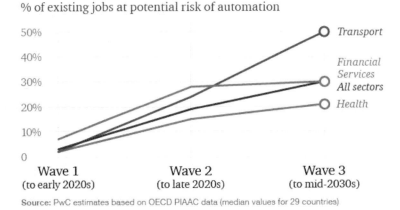

% of existing jobs at potential risk of automation

Source: PwC estimates based on OECD PIAAC data (median values for 29 countries)

PWC describes these waves as:

(1) *The algorithm wave:* automation of simple computational tasks and analysis of structured data in areas like finance, information and communications – already well underway.

(2) *The augmentation wave:* automation of repeatable tasks such as filling in forms, communicating and exchanging information through dynamic

[1] C.B. Frey, & M.A. Osborne, *The Future of Employment: How Susceptible are Jobs to Computerization?*, Oxford University Press, 2013.

[2] 35% equals just over 11 million jobs.

[3] Will robots really steal our jobs?, PWC

technological support, and statistical analysis of unstructured data in semi-controlled environments such as aerial drones and robots in warehouses – also underway, but likely to come to maturity in the 2020s.

(3) *The autonomy wave:* automation of physical labour and manual dexterity, and problem solving in dynamic real-world situations that require responsive actions, such as in manufacturing and transport (e.g. driverless vehicles) – technologies are under development already, but may only come to full maturity in the 2030s.

PWC expresses the view that ten million British workers are at risk of losing their jobs as a result of the revolution, although the OECD[1] has indicated that the UK may be less affected than other countries which have a larger manufacturing base.[2] A commonly held view is the most affected areas will be transportation and storage (with over 50% of jobs potentially lost), manufacturing (45%), construction (35%), wholesale and retail (30%) with public administration and defence also at 30%.

The OECD has warned that its member countries are failing to prepare workers for a revolution *that will leave 66 million people at risk of being replaced by machines in the coming years*. It also reported that the most vulnerable workers *were less likely to be receiving help than those whose jobs were more secure*. In other words, companies will no doubt train or re-train those (few) they intend to keep, but no help will be available for the rest.

> *The insecurity that automation brings will soon demand the comprehensive replacement of a benefits system that does almost nothing to encourage people to acquire new skills, and works on the expectation that it can shove anyone who's jobless into exactly the kind of work that's under threat.*[3]

Such a worry is behind the idea of a universal basic income, replacing clumsy benefits schemes with a system of paying everyone a regular sum to cover living costs, with no requirement to work or to look for work (which of course may not in be there.) The biggest worry is that those who own the

---

[1] *Automation, skills us and training*, Organisation for Economic Co-operation and Development.
[2] China may be the hardest hit.
[3] OECD *Ibid*.

automated organisations will benefit hugely while others will fall into poverty, as happened in the nineteenth century. Harris calls this *the really terrifying part.*:

> *Given that [job loss] will be disproportionately concentrated on low-wage, low-skill employment, this wave of automation inevitably threatens to worsen inequality.*[1]

As the PWC report says:

> *Governments and business need to work together to help people adjust to these new technologies through retraining and career changes. A culture of adaptability and lifelong learning will be crucial for spreading the benefits of AI and robotics widely through society, particularly with an ageing population where we need people to be able to work for longer.*

That surely includes us. Surely we are not going to repeat the error of masonic leadership in the first half of the nineteenth century and do nothing.

Not that bad?

A distinction is made between job and task, that some parts (tasks) of a job may be automated but other parts (tasks) not. An OECD report says:

> *Since occupations usually consist of performing a bundle of tasks not all of which may be easily automatable the potential for automating entire occupations and workplaces may be much lower than suggested.*[2]

A job in which more than 70% of the tasks will be automated can be said to be at risk. Using this criterion, the average job loss in OECD countries will be about 9%. (Korea lowest with 6%, Austria highest with 12%.) The variation is caused by different current investment in automation and in education of workers. The USA is right on the average at 9% while the UK is just above it at 10%. The conclusion of the task-based report is that automation may not destroy as large a number of jobs as first thought, but:

> *... low qualified workers are [still] likely to bear the brunt ... as the automatibility of their jobs is higher compared to highly qualified workers. Therefore, the likely challenge*

---

[1] John Harris, 'Ten million British jobs could be gone in 15 years. No one knows what happens next.' *Guardian*, April 2018.

[2] Arntz, M., T. Gregory and U. Zierahn (2016), 'The Risk of Automation for Jobs in OECD Countries: A Comparative Analysis', OECD Social, Employment and Migration Working Papers, No. 189, OECD Publishing, Paris.

for the future lies in coping with rising inequality and ensuring sufficient (re-)training especially for low qualified workers.

In the UK, 55% of workers occupying the lowest third of pay rates are most at risk. (USA 50%.) In the middle third, perhaps most relevant for freemasonry, 21% in the UK, (25% in USA) are predicted to lose their jobs. Thus, if all of our working members were in this middle category, one in five (UK) or one in four (USA) working masons would need to find other work. The OECD is not optimistic about this:

> ... *regaining the competitive advantage over machines by means of upskilling and training may be difficult to achieve, especially since the speed of the current technological revolution appears to exceed the pace of its predecessors.*

Our responsibility

Even on the more optimistic task-based scenario we face another perfect storm. We need to identify the income category of our brethren to estimate the size of our task, and identify what skills brethren will need to re-gain employment.[1] We need to re-build the education and skills levels of our brethren to help them adjust; get involved in job creation; and enhance our social safety net to support those who cannot adjust. We used to have a hospital to help sick brethren. We will soon need a facility to help redundant brethren. New jobs were eventually created by the Industrial Revolution:

> *By 1899, over half the members were employees, many with jobs unheard of a hundred years before: insurance agent, station master, salesman, broker and advertising agent.*

The result of the new revolution may produce a similar result. Jobs may be created which are unheard of today. The world may look very different. One list of new jobs sounds like science fiction, but the future may be just that. It should not be necessary to ask if this is really our responsibility. Brotherly love and relief demand this of us and we would be fail to be true to our brethren if we ignored it, but first we must repair our current state of membership, a matter which I discuss next.

---

[1] Many of our current members are retired and will not be much affected, but if we are to survive as an order, we will need to recruit younger, working members who will be.

85

A certain trumpet

The middle class was habit forming. We became hooked on it as a recruitment source. The fact that prior to the 1950s middle class candidates came along in a steady stream, meant that we never had to question what we are, analyse our values or decide what we offer to society. We just took it for granted that we had values – without ever being forced to articulate or justify the claim. Now, when we need to be positive in the face of attacks on freemasonry, we appear uncertain, incapable of articulating our values and our place in society. We have become defensive, seeking merely to placate our detractors and respond to challenges by saying what we are **not**.

*Freemasonry is **not** a religion.*
*Freemasonry does **not** offer any path to salvation.*
*We have **no** dogma or theology.*
*Freemasonry today is **not** a whites only organisation.*
*We make **no** political statements.*

Our penalties are purely symbolic; they are **not** real.[1] We do **not** use the name of the god Ba'al.[2] We **no longer** use the word *Jabulon*.[3] We add convoluted clauses to the ceremonies of initiation, passing and raising. We even translate our three grand principles into politically correct words. The website of the United Grand Lodge of England begins with negatives:

*Freemasonry is one of the world's oldest and largest **non**-religious, **non**-political, fraternal and charitable organisations.*

The site then tells us that freemasonry teaches *self-knowledge through participation in a progression of ceremonies* and that our values are *integrity, kindness, and honesty,*

---

[1] No one thought they were.

[2] The word *Ba'al* means *master* and could be applied to any god, or indeed boss. The biblical Ba'al was a god widely worshipped in Canaan, as was his consort Asherah. There is a reputable theory that Ba'al was worshipped along with El and Yahweh in early Israel/Judah religion. See *Masonic Legends*, David West & Matthew West, Hamilton House, 2018. The story of Ba'al, Yahweh and Elijah is of course myth.

3 There is a theory that the original word was זבולון *zevulun*, probably meaning *glorious dwelling place*, appropriate given its physical location in the RA ritual. The current ritual commits the sojourners to discovering a word that did not exist until the 13th century CE.

comments sufficiently anodyne as to be untrue. Such PR-driven language seeks to persuade the public to believe that freemasonry is **not** really important; **not** really serious; **nothing** to worry about – as if we roll up our trouser legs for a laugh. Rank-and-file freemasons squirm uncomfortably in their seats when one of the rulers of the Craft tells them that freemasonry is **just** a hobby. They don't know what to think: either the speaker means what he says and has different values from them, or he is just toeing an unwelcome party line. Either way, embarrassment is the result. Most of us see freemasonry as a way of life.

A certain trumpet

Frightened by unwise PR advice, we have avoided the 'big' statement, and this simply won't do. Father Theodore Hesburgh,[1] President of Notre Dame University, argued that leadership demands a clear vision. You cannot blow an uncertain trumpet, he said, referring to Paul's *Epistle to the Corinthians*:

For if the trumpet give an uncertain sound, who shall prepare himself to the battle? [2]

We need a clear trumpet call: one that says clearly what freemasonry is and what we stand for.[3] Given a clear statement, the public can agree or disagree with us but at least they will not rely on gossip, rumour or slander for information. A positive declaration will enable the ordinary freemason to argue his corner. As things stand, the ordinary mason is dissuaded from entering into discussion, told to leave such matters to those skilled in PR. That is plain silly. The important discussions go on in the pub, at the golf club, in the gym or on the terraces.

On the next page is an draft of a 'big' statement or charter. It emphasises that we are a moral order. It shows what candidates can expect of us and what we seek to achieve in society. It provides criteria by which society may judge us and by which we can judge ourselves.

---

[1] During the 35 years he was president, he increased the operating budget from $9.7 million to $176.6 million, endowments from $9 million to $350 million, and research funding from $735,000 to $15 million. Student numbers doubled to 10,000. Football matters at American universities: during his tenure, the *Fighting Irish* won 82% of their games.

[2] 1 *Corinthians* 14:8

[3] Saying *Enough is enough* is probably not enough.

Freemasonry is a moral practice. We enable good men to live respected and die regretted.

There are periodic intervals in human experience when the moral life comes under attack. Now is such a time, and we must respond.

We will become a reservoir of social capital, enabling society to preserve the virtue of trust. We will provide a bastion for the virtues in an amoral world, maintaining a community within which the moral life is lived.

In choosing to become a freemason, a man accepts an obligation to live according to the virtues of the order. Such a choice cannot be made lightly.

There is no sense in which a man can say, 'I want to be a freemason but not a good one.'

To be a freemason is to exhibit specific virtues. The most important of these are the three grand principles – brotherly love, relief and truth – and the four cardinal virtues – prudence, fortitude, temperance, and justice.

The great role that I propose for freemasonry is the preservation of the moral life, becoming a bastion for the defence of the trust. To describe this role, I need to take you through some moral philosophy. I will do my best to minimise the technical jargon but I cannot avoid it altogether, so some parts of the following chapters may be heavy going. This overview may help.

Overview – philosophical argument

Philosophers have shown that we cannot derive a moral statement (an *ought*) from a factual statement (an *is*.) This often referred to as the *ought/is distinction* and it dates from the time of David Hume (1711–1776).

> *In every system of morality, which I have hitherto met with, I have always remarked, that the author proceeds for some time in the ordinary way of reasoning, and establishes the being of a God, or makes observations concerning human affairs; when of a sudden I am surprised to find, that instead of the usual copulations of propositions, is, and is not, I meet with no proposition that is not connected with an ought, or an ought not. This change is imperceptible; but is, however, of the last consequence. For as this ought, or ought not, expresses some new relation or affirmation, 'tis necessary that it should be observed and explained; and at the same time that a reason should be given, for what seems altogether inconceivable, how this new relation can be a deduction from others, which are entirely different from it.*[1]

So if not from facts, how are moral statements derived? Some writers have sought the justification of morality in religion; that certain actions are right or wrong because a god has said they are. There are philosophical arguments against such a theory but in any case people who have no religion can and do make moral judgements and so religion cannot be the only basis of morality.

Some philosophers and many ordinary people hold that moral statements are just expressions of our feelings, a theory known in philosophy as *emotivism*. However, we do justify our moral judgements by argument, using examples and precedents, not something we normally do with feelings. What is more, without the prior existence of morality, we could not refer to those many emotions which are described in moral terms, for example, pride, indignation, patriotism and contrition.

Jean-Paul Sartre (1905–1980) argued that we must not accept morality as merely tradition or habit: doing certain things because they are socially acceptable or avoiding certain actions because our parents told us to. Sartre

---

[1] *Treatise of Human Nature*, 1738. Penguin Classics, ed. Ernest Mossner, 1985.

argues that to be *authentic*, a moral judgement must be rational and made by ourselves. He says that in deciding whether an action is right or wrong, we define ourselves,[1] that in accepting *thus and such* an action, we become the person who thinks *thus and such* is acceptable. The criterion of *authenticity* helps to remind us that morality is more than habit.

The tradition of the virtues that stems from Aristotle[2] does not start from facts. It assumes a *purpose-to-life*, which is itself a moral statement. *Life is all about …* is not a factual statement but the first part of a value judgement. The whole form of such a judgement is: *Life is all about … therefore we must …* If we can ascertain and describe a purpose-to-life, we can generate a moral life from it. Such a purpose-to-life would be dependent upon its *context*. What a warrior hero might see as important in life would be different from a religious hermit's view.

Thus we *choose* a purpose-to-life with a morality that derives from it, and thereby define ourselves as people who accept that form of moral life. If carried out rationally and after due consideration, such a choice will still be *authentic* in Sartre's terms. Those who choose to live by the *Rule of St Benedict* define themselves as Benedictines, much more than a name. To be a Benedictine is to *choose* to live by the Rule.[3]

The moral life is in danger because it seems impossible today to find an existing socially agreed context, a purpose-to-life, which can support it. However, on a parallel with St Benedict and his rule, I will argue that freemasonry can offer one. I will go further than this and argue that safeguarding the moral life must become the function of our order, because freemasonry is one of very few institutions today that can do it. It is also the way that we will save ourselves.

---

[1] This is part of what is known as *existentialism*.

[2] *Nicomachean Ethics*, Penguin Classics, 2004.

[3] The use of the words *purpose-to-life* is dangerous. I should like you to think of it as a technical term and so have added hyphens. I do not mean to imply that there is only one purpose-to-life.

Values and relativity

November 2010

One Barclays trader wrote in a chatroom: *If you ain't cheating, you ain't trying.*[1]

November 2014

In one of the darkest days in the histories of the City and Wall Street, six major banks were fined a total of £2.6 billion ($4.10bn) by regulators. A seventh, Barclays, is still in talks over the size of its penalty. The punishments came after an inquiry by watchdogs in Britain, the US and Switzerland into rigging of the foreign-exchange market. Over £3 trillion ($4.75trn) is traded daily on the international currency market, and the banks' traders were found to have manipulated prices.

What was shocking, even by the standards of the scandals of the past few years, was what regulators portrayed as the arrogance of the bank employees. They formed groups and gave themselves nicknames such as 'The A-Team', or 'The Three Musketeers'. They communicated with each other via chatrooms. One HSBC trader complained in an email to another team member who had not given him the information he needed: *You are useless ... how can I make free money with no fcking* [sic] *heads up.*

The report, by Britain's Financial Conduct Authority, laid bare the contempt in which some bank employees hold their banks, colleagues and clients. But what is especially shaming was that the manipulation occurred recently – after a series of scandals which resulted in banks paying enormous fines and employees losing their jobs. This gives the lie to the claim by the banking community they were reforming their ways and were doing everything they could to prevent misdemeanours.[2]

May 2015

Citi, JPMorgan, Barclays, RBS, Bank of America and UBS will pay almost $6 billion to authorities, bringing the total fines over the FX scandal to $9 billion. In a particularly embarrassing twist, the forex charges come right on the heels of the Libor interest rate scandal, where banks were found to be rigging the rates.

Near-criminal behaviour

It has been said that Ivan Boesky (of *greed is good* fame) wore a T-shirt emblazoned with the words, *He who has the most when he dies, wins.* If true, it partly explains the City of London's near criminal behaviour. The money the traders made was a badge of victory, a scoreline; nothing real or of enduring value. They lived in a nonsense world. I was once told by the UK head of

[1] *Independent*, May 21 2015.
[2] Chris Blackhurst, *The Independent*, 13 November 2014.

Moët Hennessy Louis Vuitton that less than half of their champagne was drunk; the rest was poured over people in celebrations. The world of the trader is as artificial as the champagne. Simon English writes:

> *The unofficial offer from the bank that employs the traders is this: here are a series of rules we take very seriously. Try to get around them without getting caught. If you make a bundle, we'll give you a slice. If you lose it, well, that's unauthorised dealing. Best of luck.*[1]

Greed (avarice, covetousness or cupidity) is, of course, one of the seven deadly sins. In Dante's *The Divine Comedy*, the greedy souls suffering torment in the fourth circle of hell learn that *not all the gold that is beneath the moon* can purchase rest for them.[2] St Thomas Aquinas wrote that greed is:

> *… a sin directly against one's neighbour, since one man cannot over-abound in external riches without another man lacking them, for temporal goods cannot be possessed by many at the same time … It is a sin against God, just as are all mortal sins, inasmuch as man views things eternal with contempt, preferring temporal things.*[3]

Would Boesky, or for that matter the *A-Team* and the *Three Musketeers*, be brought up short by what the saint said? None of them would give a damn, to use an appropriate pun. For Boesky that *temporal goods cannot be possessed by many at the same time* was just the point. The CEO of one broking firm said:

> *Blaming traders for being greedy and manipulative … when you put temptation in their way, is like putting a fox in charge of a hen coop and then expressing surprise about the outcome.*[4]

The trading took place in a moral vacuum. While there may be a distorted echo of ethics in the question, *How can I make free money with no fcking heads up?* any genuine moral judgement on their actions would have meant little to

---

[1] Simon English, *Evening Standard*, November 2014. His description of a trader is fascinating: *He was brilliant at knowing why* [the bonds] *would move and when. He made clients and himself oodles of money. After a while something became clear. He didn't know much about anything other than German bonds. He had never been to Germany and hadn't the slightest interest in going. He thought the capital was Frankfurt.*

[2] *Inferno*, Canto VII.

[3] Aquinas *Summa Theoligica* II, Section 11, Ave Maria Press, 2000.

[4] Terry Smith, CEO of Tullett Prebon.

them. Their world builds a wall around itself and becomes a morality-free zone. There is, after all, no point in accusing a fox of greed or cruelty.

> *The culture of the trading floor is worse than any media commentator, author or film can depict and nothing, absolutely nothing has changed since the banking crisis. These guys think they are untouchable. It's a pervasive culture where if your face fits, you're in and it's tolerated by the guys at the top because the traders bring in such vast commissions and profits.*[1]

Psychopaths

The behaviour of traders is similar to that of psychopaths. Often thought of as the most dangerous of human beings, a psychopath[2] has no conscience and is incapable of experiencing gratitude, guilt, remorse or shame. Psychopaths are incapable of living the moral life. They have no compunction about cheating and lying. When found out, they will express surprise and regret, make apologies and then repeat the crime.

> [They] *will commit theft, forgery, adultery, fraud, and other deeds for astonishingly small stakes and under much greater risks of being discovered than will the ordinary scoundrel.*[3]

They can mimic normal behaviour and can be very convincing. They can charm others into thinking they are decent and reliable. They use people. The criminologist, David Wilson, describes psychopaths as *hiding in plain sight*. Around one per cent of the UK population are psychopaths and they can and do function in organisations.[4] Being charming to those above them but abusive to those below, they are more commonly found at higher levels of the hierarchy and figures of three to four percent have been suggested for more senior positions in business.[5] There is no reason to believe that they do not exist at higher levels in freemasonry.

---

[1] English, *op. cit.*

[2] The word *psychopath* was replaced by *sociopath* and then by *people with Antisocial Personality Disorder.* I have kept the original word because it is used in the works I have quoted from.

[3] Hervey Cleckley, *The Mask of Sanity*, Literary Licensing LLC, 2011, (first pub. by The CV Mosby Company, 1941).

[4] David Wilson, 'How psychopaths hide in plain sight – a psychological analysis of serial killer Dennis Rader', *Independent*, 18 August 2015.

[5] Robert D. Hare, *Psychopathy: Theory and Research*, John Wiley & Sons Inc., 1970.

A study carried out by Thomas Noll *et al.* indicates that competition motivates traders more than financial gain. In pursuit of competitive advantage, they are ruthless and willing to harm others. Using a version of the game, the *Prisoners Dilemma*,[1] Noll discovered:

> ... *the traders used an even more uncooperative strategy than the psychopaths, maximizing their relative gain only by harming the game partner. This result ... is surprising in view of the fact that traders are supposed to maximize the total gain for their businesses. By jeopardizing their total gain only to improve the relative gain, the traders seem to be motivated more by competition than by lucrative pragmatism.*[2]

The psychopath cannot appreciate other people's needs[3] and the trader simply wants to win. Traders are isolated from the moral life, while psychopaths are incapable of living it. In neither case would persuasion have any effect in getting them to change their ways. If someone does not live the moral life, there is no way that we can prove that they ought to.

Ought and *is*

I present this as psychology but it is also about logic. Take four statements, similar in content but differing in overtones.

A. *That act will in all probability result in the death of a human being.*
B. *You will kill someone with that car.*
C. *You were drunk and you ran him over.*
D. *You murdered him.*

Statement A seems to be simply a statement of fact; the speaker informing the listener that an act being considered carries a certain result. Nevertheless, the wording is stilted, as if seeking to suppress overtones.

---

[1] The *Prisoners' Dilemma* itself was developed by Merrill Flood and Melvin Dresher. The police have arrested two suspects who they think worked together to commit a crime. If both remain silent under interrogation, the police cannot hold them for lack of evidence. If only one talks, the silent one will receive a stiffer sentence and the one who turns state's evidence will receive a lighter one. If both confess neither gain any advantage.

[2] Noll, Thomas et al., 'A Comparison of Professional Traders and Psychopaths in a Simulated Non-Zero Sum Game', *Catalyst*, Vol. 2, Issue 2, 2012.

[3] Psychopaths are quite different from people with autism. An autistic person may have difficulty in understanding that others have emotions and may appear uncaring. Unlike psychopaths, autistic people do value others and can learn to respond appropriately.

Statement B seems similar but the overtones are now obvious. They are carried by the personalisation of *you*, the use of the word *kill*, and the phrase *that car*, the implication being that the car is not maintained or is capable of speeds beyond the skill of the driver.

Statement C is tantamount to a moral accusation. The statement might be that of a judge giving sentence.

Statement D is a moral judgement. The word *murder* means wrongful killing and so the evaluation is contained in the meaning. The question in a court of law is not whether murder is wrong (which is a tautology) but whether the act of the accused counts as murder.[1]

The overtones show our moral sense at work. Most of us would say that if an action *is likely* to cause the death of a human being, it *ought to* be prevented. However, there is no logical connection between the statement:

That act will in all probability cause the death of a human being

and the moral conclusion:

If you can prevent that act, you ought to do so.

Another step is required:

Statement A	*That act will in all probability cause the death of a human being.*
Extra step	*Causing the death of a human being is wrong.*
Conclusion	*If you can prevent that act, you ought to do so.*

It is a mark of a moral agent that he or she consciously or unconsciously adds that extra step, but psychopaths would hear no overtones, nor would the extra step register with them.

> *The presence or absence of conscience is a deep human division … What distinguishes [psychopaths] from the rest of us is an utterly empty hole in the psyche, where there should be the most evolved of all humanizing functions.*[2]

The psychopath has no conscience while the trader's has been suppressed.

---

[1] Sir Edward Coke (d. 1634), the greatest of early jurists, wrote: *Murder is when a man of sound memory and of the age of discretion, unlawfully killeth … any reasonable creature in rerum natura under the King's peace, with malice aforethought …*

[2] Martha Stout, *The Sociopath Next Door*, Broadway Books, 2005.

Emotivism

Since it seems impossible to convince anyone to lead the moral life if they do not do so already, some philosophers have taken moral statements to be no more than an expression of feelings. It is after all common enough for someone asked for justification of a moral position to reply, *I don't know. I just feel that …* According to the theory of emotivism, the statement *Causing people unnecessary pain is wrong*, expresses a negative feeling, something like *Boo! to causing people unnecessary pain*. The statement *It is a duty to help others in distress*, expresses a positive feeling, something like *Hooray for helping others in distress!* and the statement *You ought to help people in distress* is no more than encouragement to share the feeling, something like *Shout hooray for helping others in distress!* [1]

Moral persuasion

Charles Stevenson's treatment of the theory contains many valuable insights, particularly in his treatment of moral persuasion. It is often true that:

> *A redirection of the hearer's attitudes is sought not by the mediating step of altering his beliefs, but by exhortation, whether obvious or subtle, crude or refined.*

Redirection of attitudes is accomplished by:

> *… emotive meaning, rhetorical cadence, apt metaphor, stentorian, stimulating, or pleading tones of voice, dramatic gestures, … establishing rapport with the hearer or audience …* [2]

Great speech makers from Cicero[3] to Martin Luther King[4] have aroused emotions in this way but a problem for Stevenson's theory is that the emotions aroused are described in moral terms. (The words that follow in italics carry the moral force.) Cicero sought to arouse feelings of *shame* in Lucius Sergius Catilina (Catiline) and *righteous anger* in the Senate at Catiline's attempt to *overthrow democracy* in Rome.

---

[1] I use ! as a marker, showing the statement to be an expression of emotion.

[2] Charles L. Stevenson, *Ethics and Language*, Yale University Press, 1944.

[3] *When, O Catiline, will you cease abusing our patience? How long is that madness of yours still to mock us?*

[4] *I have a dream that one day this nation will rise up and live out the true meaning of its creed. 'We hold these truths to be self-evident, that all men are created equal.'*

Martin Luther King sought both to arouse *shame* in the American population at their *selective memory* of Abraham Lincoln's 1863 executive order on *emancipation* and to *stiffen the resolve* of black Americans in their *fight for equality*. Winston Churchill successfully aroused the *patriotism* of the British people and motivated them to make the *necessary sacrifices* in preparation for a *Nazi invasion* that every Briton in June 1940 believed to be imminent.[1]

A redirection of the hearer's moral attitudes can often be achieved by exhortation but the emotions that are being redirected are moral emotions: *shame, righteous anger, stiffening of resolve, patriotism, necessary sacrifices* and so on. To describe the emotions aroused, we need to use the moral terms first. (A philosopher might say the moral terms are *logically anterior* to the emotion.)

The logic of emotion

No doubt physical feelings are associated with shame (hot flushes, perhaps) but the feelings are not the emotion itself. There are logical and grammatical requirements for the use of many emotion words. To experience shame, one or someone close to one has to have done something wrong, just as to feel pride, one or someone close to one has to have done something well. That is the meaning of the words. It would not be just psychologically odd, but logically odd to say one felt shame at having done something praiseworthy.

Suppose the traditional *Poor Old Lady* (*POL*) is taken ill, requiring help which a friend of ours does not give. If our friend were to say, *I am feeling really bad about not helping said POL,* we might well reply, *Well, so you ought.* We would not recommend an aspirin but rather suggest some act of penitence. The pain of remorse is logically different from the pain of a headache. The latter is a sensation, the former a confession. When talking about shame, we are talking about morals as well as feelings.

Living the moral life is about attributing value to the world. Valuing is

---

[1] *Even though large tracts of Europe and many old and famous States have fallen or may fall into the grip of the Gestapo and all the odious apparatus of Nazi rule, we shall not flag or fail. We shall go on to the end. We shall fight in France. We shall fight on the seas and oceans. We shall fight with growing confidence and growing strength in the air. We shall defend our Island, whatever the cost may be. We shall fight on the beaches. We shall fight on the landing grounds. We shall fight in the fields and in the streets. We shall fight in the hills. We shall never surrender.*

something we do. Emotion comes in because we have feelings about what we value. A proof that someone genuinely holds values is that they are upset if such values are transgressed. Values are not themselves part of the world. Wittgenstein wrote:

> *In the world everything is as it is and happens as it does happen. In it there is no value – and if there were, it would be of no value.* [1]

Adjectives such as *blue, shiny, tall, long, scary, late* or *smooth* describe qualities of things in the world, while adjectives such as *dignified, proper, handsome, beautiful, ugly, good, bad, right* or *wrong* are evaluations of them. Aesthetic judgements operate in much the same way. In the description of a sunset, the word *beautiful* does not further the description so much as evaluate the sight. [2]

Arbitrariness

The fact that it may be impossible to convince someone of a moral or aesthetic judgement, does not mean that discussions of moral or aesthetic issues are irrational. In fact, it is common that opposing views in a moral debate are supported by evidence. Take the example of war.

Some people argue that wars in foreign countries are none of our business and that intervention makes things worse. Others hold that developed democracies are morally required to minimise bloodshed in less developed countries. [3] Still others hold that no war can be right because holy books say that killing people is wrong, while others hold that there are religious justifications for war. Jonathan Riley-Smith writes of the Crusades:

> *All Christian justifications of positive violence are based partly on the belief that a particular religious or political system or course of political events is one in which Christ is intimately involved ... If the only way to preserve the integrity of his intentions from those who stand in their way is to use force, then this is in accordance with his desires.* [4]

---

[1] Ludwig Wittgenstein, *Tractatus Logico-Philosophicus*, trnsl. D.F. Pears & B.F. McGuinness, Routledge, 1961, first published 1921.

[2] Although since we know what sunsets most people think are beautiful, we more or less know what one called beautiful looks like.

[3] Of course whether interventions make things worse can in theory be factually determined.

[4] Jonathan Riley-Smith, 'Revival and Survival', in Riley-Smith (ed.) *The Oxford History of the Crusades*, Oxford University Press, 1999.

Utilitarianism argues that wars are just if the happiness to be gained outweighs the pain done. The use of atomic bombs on Japan in 1945 might be justified by the reduction in the number of deaths of Allied soldiers[1] but, then again, John Donne wrote:

Who bends not his ear to any bell which upon occasion rings? … No man is an island, entire of itself; every man is a piece of the continent, a part of the main … any man's death diminishes me, because I am involved in mankind, and therefore never send to know for whom the bells tolls; it tolls for thee.[2]

The best way to ensure peace, we are told, is to prepare for war. Not only should our nation arm itself, it must show that it is prepared to use its armaments. *Mutually Assured Destruction* (**MAD**) ensures nuclear peace. On the other hand, the Campaign for Nuclear Disarmament argues:

Nuclear weapons have no legitimate purpose; nor would their use be legal due to civilian casualties being unavoidable … Not only do nuclear weapons kill indiscriminately but the radioactive fallout … means that their effects know no geographical boundaries.

The arguments may be presented in a reasoned way but, since there are no independent criteria for deciding which premises are correct, disagreements too easily become, as MacIntyre says, a matter of assertion and counter-assertion, and moral argument is *disquietingly arbitrary.*

Antigone

MacIntyre directs us to Sophocles' play, *Antigone*. I know the Jean Anouilh version[3] better and will refer to that. The background to the play is of two Theban brothers who have fought each other in a civil war. Both have died.

---

[1] One of the most powerful statements about Hiroshima and Nagasaki comes from George Macdonald Fraser's *Quartered Safe Out Here*, his memoir of the Burma campaign. While personally convinced that the bombing was justified, he believed that the men under his command, had they known what results the bombs had, would have gathered their gear *with moaning and foul language and ill-tempered harking back to the long dirty bloody miles from the Imphal boxes to the Sittang Bend and the iniquity of having to go again, slinging their rifles and bickering about who was to go on point, and 'Ah's aboot 'ed it, me!' and 'You, ye bugger, ye're knackered avower ye start, you!' and 'We'll a' get killed!'*, and then would have moved south to continue the war as before.

[2] Donne, John, 'Station 17, Now this bell tolling softly for another…', *Devotions upon Emergent Occasions and Death's Duel*, Vintage Spiritual Classics, 1999.

[3] *Antigone*, Random House, 1946.

Créon, the new ruler of Thebes, decides that to regain peace, the populace need to see that good has triumphed and evil has been punished. He decides that one of the dead brothers will be a hero and the other traitor:

Jean Anouilh in 1971

I had the prettier of the two carcasses brought in and gave it a state funeral; and I left the other to rot. I don't know which was which. And I assure you, I don't care.

Contrary to Créon's edict, the eponymous Antigone, sister of the two dead brothers, creeps out at night to bury the remaining corpse, and is arrested. The dramatic centre of the play is the face-to-face between Créon and Antigone, the former arguing that what he has done is necessary for peace, while the latter insists that familial and religious duties require her to bury the body. Créon is the pragmatist. He sees himself as an embodiment of the law, and dislikes many of the things he has to do. He never wanted to be king but was was landed with the job after the civil war. Chorus says at the start of the play:

I'll tell you something about Créon. Now and then, when he goes to bed weary with the day's work, he wonders whether this business of being a leader of men is worth the trouble.

He doesn't see kingship as romantic:

It is my trade; a trade a man has to work at every day; and like every other trade, it isn't all beer and skittles. But since it is my trade, I take it seriously.

Antigone is often seen as the idealist, someone for whom any compromise in her ethical and religious ideals is anathema. She is ready-made martyr material. Chorus says of her at the beginning of the play:

All that she knows is that Créon won't allow her dead brother to be buried; and that despite Créon, she must bury him ... Antigone doesn't think, she acts; she doesn't reason, she feels, and from the moment the curtain went up, she began to feel that inhuman forces were whirling her out of this world.

The stand-off between Créon and Antigone is a perfect example of two contexts with no contact.

Créon:	*Why did you try to bury your brother?*
Antigone:	*I owed it to him.*
Créon:	*I had forbidden it.*
Antigone:	*I owed it to him. Those who are not buried wander eternally and find no rest. Everybody knows that. If my brother were alive and he came home weary after a long day's hunting, I should fetch him food and drink and see that his bed was ready for him. Polynices is home from the hunt. I owe it to him to unlock the house of the dead in which my father and my mother are waiting to welcome him. Polynices has earned his rest.*
Créon:	*Polynices was a rebel and a traitor, and you know it.*
Antigone:	*He was my brother.*
Créon:	*You heard my edict. It was proclaimed throughout Thebes. You read my edict. It was posted up on the city walls.*
Antigone:	*Yes. Of course I did.*
Créon:	*You knew the punishment I decreed for any person who attempted to give him burial.*
Antigone:	*Yes, I knew the punishment.*

Créon's argument that both brothers were a bad lot and both deserved to be executed for treason, does not move Antigone, but he makes a last appeal:

Don't think that I am not just as offended as you are by the thought of that meat rotting in the sun. In the evening, when the breeze comes in off the sea, you can smell it in the palace, and it nauseates me. … It's vile; and I can tell you what I wouldn't tell anybody else: it's stupid, monstrously stupid. But the people of Thebes have got to have their noses rubbed into it a little longer.

Antigone refuses to compromise and tells Créon that if he leaves her alive, she will bury her brother again. Who wins? No one, of course. Antigone's sister, Ismène, declares that she too will bury her brother. Antigone crows:

Antigone: *You hear that, Créon? The thing is catching! Who knows but that lots of people will catch the disease from me! What are you waiting for? Call in your guards! Come on, Créon! Show a little courage! It only hurts for a minute!*

It is not a fun ending. Complicating matters is Antigone's engagement to Créon's son, Haemon. Antigone is walled up alive and Haemon goes in with her. Realising this, Créon calls for the wall to be knocked down but Antigone has hung herself and Haemon has killed himself with his sword. Créon then receives the news that his wife has cut her throat:

Créon: *She, too? They are all asleep. It must be good to sleep.* [To Page.] *My lad.*

Page: *Sir?*

Créon: *Listen to me. They don't know it but the truth is the work is there to be done and a man can't fold his arms and refuse to do it. They say it's dirty work but if we didn't do it, who would?*

Page. *I don't know, sir.*

Créon: *Of course you don't. You'll be lucky if you never find out. In a hurry to grow up aren't you?*

Page: *Oh yes, sir.*

Créon: *I shouldn't be if I were you. Never grow up if you can help it. What time is it?*

Page: *Five o'clock, sir.*

Créon: *What do we have on today at five o'clock?*

Page: *Cabinet meeting, sir.*

Créon: *Cabinet meeting. Then we had better go along to it.*

Who was right?

You may think that Antigone's resistance to compromise is admirable, that she is right to stick to her ideals of familial and religious duty. You may think that what Créon did was necessary, a matter of politics, the art of the possible. You may also think that Créon was an *apparatchik*, willing to compromise moral demands for the needs of the situation. You may also think that Antigone was a spoilt brat. I suppose that all these views are true and that is the power of the play. It is said that when Anouilh's version was first produced in Paris in 1944,[1] the Nazi authorities sided with Créon and the French saw Antigone as a heroine of the resistance. That view was certainly denied by *Le Populaire*, in its review by Guy Desson on 30 September 1944: *Antigone n'est pas davantage le symbole de la Résistance que Créon l'apologie de la dictature.*[2] Most commentators agree that Créon and Antigone are equally balanced and that is the point. Anouilh shows us how two opposing moral positions can lead to tragedy.

Morality and interpretation

It is often said that all we need to do is to *teach children the difference between right and wrong*; that everyone knows that murder is wrong and so is stealing, lying and swearing. Such statements are tautologies: the truth is contained in their meaning. Like murder, stealing is defined as wrong. The *Theft Act* 1968 starts:

> *A person is guilty of theft if he dishonestly appropriates property belonging to another with the intention of permanently depriving the other of it.*

While we might tell a child *lying is wrong*, such a form of moral statement is rare in normal discourse. Moral issues often arise as matters of interpretation:

> *I'd vote for hanging. Doesn't everyone occasionally pay cash to avoid VAT? Surely it doesn't matter if I exceed the speed limit a bit when I'm in a hurry. There's such a thing as a white lie, you know. Finders, keepers. If someone said that to my wife, I'd give him a good hiding. People who stop on every amber just hold up traffic.*

It is the interpretation that matters. Is hanging a form of murder? When is a lie a white lie? Can you really keep money you find in the street – and does the amount make a difference? Personally, I find it objectionable to be offered a cash price to avoid VAT but a close friend thinks I am far too picky. Another friend likes fast cars and drives them fast. Can we really take the law into our own hands? While someone might not cheat a family member, he or

---

[1] In fact there were two opening nights for the play: the first under the Nazi occupation in February 1944, and the second after the liberation in September. Jean-Louis Barsacq, *Place Dancourt*, Gallimard, 2005.

[2] 'Antigone is no more the symbol of the Resistance than Créon the apologist for the dictatorship.'

she may have fewer reservations about cheating a stranger. While people may avoid lying to their friends, they may well be ready to lie when employed to sell or advertise products, even seeing it as their job to do so.

No list of commandments could even begin to approach the resolution of such moral issues – although effective sermons might be preached on them. What we learn from the *The A-Team*, psychopaths, emotivism, *Antigone* and the apparent arbitrariness of moral judgements, is that discussion about them cannot take place unless both disputants admit of the moral life, but that even when they do, gaining agreement is very difficult.

To be a participant in the moral life is to have decided that some things matter. The question is what things? On what can we base our moral decisions? To what criteria can we appeal?

Holy books and moral decisions

We say in the ritual:

> As a freemason, I would first recommend to your most serious contemplation the Volume of the Sacred Law, charging you to consider it the unerring standard of truth and justice and to regulate your actions by the Divine precepts it contains.

In practice, it never has been that simple and it is not often that an appeal to a holy book resolves a moral question. Consider the failures to resolve questions about contraception, abortion, assisted dying, stem cells, blood transfusions, women bishops or lesbian, gay and transgender issues, even within one religion and using one book.

Reference to a holy book is even less useful today, because there are many different books in use and because a growing number of people have no religious belief. But if religion is not the default arbiter of morality, what is? Various criteria have been suggested, the most famous being the utilitarian principle, the *greatest good for the greatest number*,[1] but none are completely satisfactory. We lack a rational basis on which to build a system of morals.

---

[1] Others include the golden rule: *Do as you would be done by;* the Kantian, *Do what you would will would become a universal rule;* and every mother's favourite, *Suppose everyone did that?*

It is characteristic of moral demands to be self-justifying.

I have to do this because it is right.

I cannot do that because it is wrong.

The reasoning is circular and the demand uncompromising. It is in the nature of ethics that conflicts are between absolutes. If I have promised to lend a book to someone, I have to fulfil the promise, even when the book actually belongs to someone else. I should not have made the promise but, having done so, I am now caught between two opposing demands, neither of which admits of compromise.

Psychology and morality

How is this?

We see and do many things during the day, only a few of which are new to us. Most of the time we operate on what one might call *automatic pilot*, from tying a shoelace to eating a sandwich. Even driving the car can be automatic.[1] We rarely decide consciously how to react to events or people. There is insufficient time to give each and every event individual attention and so our minds store experiences away in a sort of filing system, together with a package of suitable reactions of words, actions and emotions. Normally lying dormant, the relevant package is triggered by the appropriate stimulus. This explains stereotypes. We are unconscious of the existence of these packages, which psychologists call *schema*, but much of what we think, do, say and feel is caused by them.[2] The schema are laid down by our upbringing, education and social norms. Our ethical stances and beliefs are very much part of this. Such a process is not orderly. Philip Larkin wrote:

They fuck you up, your mum and dad.

They may not mean to, but they do.[3]

Our ethical system is not logically consistent because our moral decisions

---

[1] How many times have you driven home from work and had no recollection of what happened en route?

[2] Cordelia Fine, *A Mind of its Own*, Icon Books, 2007.

[3] Philip Larkin, 'This be the verse', *High Windows*, Faber & Faber, 1979.

carry baggage from our upbringing, our education and traditions – and these are not consistent with each other. It is the baggage that makes moral decision-making so hard. Because moral demands are uncompromising and because we carry incompatible moral schema, we frequently find ourselves facing insoluble moral dilemmas.

Existentialism

Existentialism effectively holds that bringing such schema to our consciousness and preventing them from making decisions for us, is the groundwork of an authentic moral life. For Jean-Paul Sartre, an authentic decision is one independent of our past, our upbringing, schooling, and experience. To be authentic demands that we surface the unconscious promptings of *what we are* and use conscious reason to choose what will define us. This is the existentialist response to the apparent arbitrariness of moral decision-making. When faced with contradictory demands, we accept neither but analyse possible courses of action and consciously choose, becoming the person who made that choice.[1] Moral decision-making requires a conscious exercise of the will.

In what follows, I will explore the idea that there is no one set of virtues admired in all societies at all times. I shall suggest that the answer to the problem of relativity of morals lies in the use of a difficult and dangerous phrase: *the purpose-to-life*. At the end of my book *Deism*, I wrote:

> *There may be no threats of hell or promises of heaven to make us good. There may be no set of laws or commandments laid down for everyone. That means we have to decide for ourselves where values lie. I cannot decide for you and you cannot decide for me, but we may both decide to share a form of life; if so, we become brothers. Explanation of this requires another book but as an introduction to it, I am in fact happy with Newton's remark that such talk is for the sake of dreams and ... fictions of our own devising, but you will note that three dots now replace the word vain.*

I hope now to explain what I mean by this.

---

[1] Sartre's socialism follows from his views on authenticity. Capitalism, colonialism, sexism and racism define people and prevent them from becoming what they would choose to be.

Morality and context

This chapter relies heavily on the insights of Alasdair MacIntyre.

Eudaimonia

Plato and Aristotle viewed ethics as the attainment of well-being (εὐδαιμονία). This is not a simple concept and the common translation of the word as happiness is misleading. To get the drift, try to combine rationality, well-being, control and success with an absence of guilt or stress. Not easy, I agree.

In an attempt to make it easier, I will adopt a masonic phrase which I think comes near to what Plato and Aristotle mean. During the installation of the Master, he is advised that by *rising to eminence by merit* [he] *may live respected and die regretted*, and I will take the attainment of the state of *living respected and dying regretted* to be similar to Aristotle's attainment of *eudaimonia*. Someone who lives respected and dies regretted is someone who has achieved admirable ends in an admirable way.

Excellences

In the ritual, the word *virtue* often appears in the singular, as in … *to the just and virtuous man, death hath no terrors equal to the stains of falsehood and dishonour.*[1] Here the word means *morally good*. The idea that different virtues matter in different times and in different social contexts may be initially surprising. However, the ritual uses the word *excellences* as a synonym of *virtues:*

> … *as a freemason, there are other excellences of character to which your attention may be particularly and forcibly directed.*

… and using the word *excellence* in place of *virtue* may help to understand what Aristotle means. It is easier to accept that certain excellences of character were required to *live respected &c.* in the context of Athens and that other excellences would be admired in other contexts. Aristotle lived 384–322 BCE in Athens, a place and time very different from our own when *to be a good man*

---

[1] This statement might well fit with Aristotle's virtue of courage.

was on every Greek view at least closely allied to being a good citizen[1] His list of virtues describe a man who *lives respected &c.* at that time and in that place, but not necessarily in any other time and place.

Aristotle's list of virtues/excellences includes:	
Courage	Experiencing fear & being sensibly cautious but neither cowardly nor rash. Facing death in a dignified & resolute manner.
Liberality	Knowing the right way to use money, being neither mean nor profligate; generous with a sense of style.
Magnificence	Being able to afford magnificent actions and substantial expenditure, perhaps endowing a new warship or temple.
High-mindedness	Sacrificing personal ease for noble purposes; neither brash nor humble, disparaging oneself being as bad as boasting.
Wittiness	Having charm, wit and tact for good conversation, enabling people to enjoy being together. Neither a bore nor a clown.
Amiability	Neither sycophantic nor ingratiating, neither presumptuous nor self-abasing, enjoying company, even at some personal expense.

The purpose to life

It is important to recognise that the excellences change with the context. By context I mean *a set of beliefs about the nature and purpose of life in a certain place and at a certain time.* What is thought of as the purpose-to-life will vary according to time or place. It is also important to remember that a statement of the purpose-to-life is a moral statement which already contains an *ought*. It is usually of the form:

The reason we are here is to … and therefore we ought to do …

The reason we are here is not a statement of fact but a moral statement.

We are here to help others and therefore we ought to assist that poor old lady.
We are here to create beauty, therefore we should ensure that statue is preserved.
We are here to praise god, therefore we should keep this day holy.

In these statements, the second clause, *and therefore we ought* or *therefore we should*, is entailed by the first, and there must be an unstated *ought* internal to the first clause, since no *ought* can be derived from an *is*. It is in this way that we

---

[1] MacIntyre *op. cit.*

overcome relativity: we accept that there can be other purposes to life but only one for our own context – and we can live only in our own context.

The phrase purpose-to-life is dangerous because it may be taken to mean that there is one external purpose to human existence: that someone 'put us here' to achieve some purpose.[1] Of course, if someone deliberately caused life in this universe, then whatever purpose that someone had in doing so would be his, her or its purpose, not ours.

Excellences in heroic societies

Alasdair MacIntyre

MacIntyre discusses the excellences of what he calls *heroic societies* in Homer's poetry of perhaps 1000 BCE, or in Norse sagas, from around 1200 CE. It is perhaps helpful to note these societies are a long way apart in time and that many societies with very different notions of the purpose-to-life existed between these dates.

From the comfort of a seat in lodge, it is not easy to put oneself in the position of a Norse *beserker* facing a shield wall, but as MacIntyre writes:

> ... *one central theme of heroic societies is also that death waits for* [all]. *Life is fragile, men are vulnerable and it is of the essence of the human situation that they are such* ... *The man therefore who does what he ought moves steadily towards his fate and his death. It is defeat and not victory that lies at the end. Understanding this is itself a virtue; indeed it is a necessary part of courage* ...

We can view the purpose-to-life in such a context as living life as if it were a story,[2] a *saga* if you like, and the man who *lives respected and dies regretted* in such

---

[1] A large number of people today still believe that someone/something caused life on this planet (and perhaps others). There was a time when such a belief was held by the majority and so formed the context of the moral life. However, since the idea of a creator god with purpose(s) for our lives has largely fallen into disuse, it is today less helpful in moral discourse.

[2] Something like this appears in Kipling. See *Masonic Legends*, David West & Matthew West.

context is one whose life becomes a tale told around future camp fires.

Honour is conferred by one's peers and without honour a man is without worth. [1]

The courage of the heroic warrior is not simply bravery but the stillness of heart with which the courageous man faces the inevitability of death when it comes – in battle, by drowning, illness (the action of some god), or even treachery – making a good end, often a song. This is exemplified in the saga, *The Life and Death of Cormac the Skald.* [2] Cormac dies in battle with a giant Scot who crushes Cormac's ribs in his death embrace. Caught under the weight of the giant's dead body, Cormac is unable to move. When at last he is found and carried aboard his ship, he makes this song:

Of yore never once did I ween it,
When I wielded the cleaver of targets,
That sickness was fated to foil me,
A fighter so hardy as I.
But I shrink not, for others must share it,
Stout shafts of the spear though they deem them,
O hard at my heart is the death pang,
Thus hopeless the bravest may die.

We can perhaps see that within such a context, strength of arm, fleetness of foot and tactical cunning might be admired in addition to courage. While we might have difficulty in thinking of these as virtues, we can perhaps understand them as excellences. A more modern version of such a context appears in the battle cry of Théoden, King of Rohan:[3]

Arise, arise, Riders of Théoden!
Fell deeds awake, fire and slaughter!
spear shall be shaken, shield be splintered,
a sword-day, a red day, ere the sun rises!
Ride now, ride now! Ride to Gondor!

---

[1] MacIntyre *op. cit.*

[2] The word *skald* means *singer* or *poet*. *The Life and Death of Cormac the Skald*, trnsl. Jane Smiley, Penguin Classics, 2001. (Written 1250–1300 CE, Icelandic author unknown.)

[3] J.R.R. Tolkien, *Return of the King*, Allen & Unwin, 1955.

and in

> *And then all the host of Rohan burst into song, and they sang as they slew, for the joy of battle was on them, and the sound of their singing that was fair and terrible came even to the City.*

The strength of Tolkien's writing enables us to imagine life in that context, and how its moral system might have worked.

Incompatible contexts

The purpose-to-life in Aristotle's Athens is incompatible with that of Théoden's Rohan or Cormac's Iceland. It is also incompatible with Christianity. In Athens, to *live respected &c.* required intelligence, personal charm and wealth, but for Christianity *it is easier for a camel to go through the eye of a needle, than for a rich man to enter into the kingdom of God.*[1] The Christian virtue of humility would have been a vice for Aristotle and for Cormac. St Paul spoke of the nine fruits of the spirit:

> *Love, joy, peace, long-suffering, gentleness, goodness, faith, meekness, temperance.*[2]

These sit uneasily alongside physical courage, success in battle, the ability to handle one's liquor, magnificence, speed of horse, high-mindedness, wit and amiability. MacIntyre writes:

> *Aristotle would certainly not have admired Jesus Christ and he would have been horrified by St Paul. … the notion of a final redemption of an almost unregenerate life has no place in Aristotle's scheme. The story of the thief on the cross is unintelligible in Aristotelian terms.*

So, to re-cap, excellences are what enables one to fulfil the (socially agreed) purpose-to-life. They are what enables a man to live well and be admired in a certain time and place, within a view in common of what matters in life.

It should be understood that there is no sense in asking what excellences a man or woman ought to exhibit *in any context*. They are all context specific.

---

[1] *Mark* 10:25, King James version.
[2] *Galatians* 5:22-23.

We live with the embers of a number of incompatible contexts. As a literate society with access to books, films, TV documentaries and historical dramas, we are aware of many contexts in a way that no earlier society has been, and can be drawn towards excellences from often competing contexts.

- from Christianity: *chastity, forgiveness, poverty, the reward of heaven.*
- from rationalism: *the greatest good for the greatest number, do as you would be done by* or Kant's dictum *Do what you can will to be a universal law.*
- from the context of manliness: *stand up for yourself, walk tall, stick out your chest, hold your head up, take responsibility.*
- from that of independence: *a man's gotta do what a man's gotta do,*[1] *never apologise and never explain, winning isn't everything but it sure beats coming second.*
- from earlier feminine contexts: *stand by your man, gentleness, nurturing.*
- from courtly behaviour: *ladies first, the gentler sex, not in front of the ladies.*

There are more modern elements: telling a man to *get in touch with his feminine side* and the saying *A woman without a man is like a fish without a bicycle.* We still retain echoes of the context of social democracy: *equality, decency, giving someone a leg up, positive discrimination, do your own thing* and *make love, not war,* even if these are currently under attack. All these elements are capable of making demands upon us and since it is the nature of moral demands to brook no disagreement, we can find ourselves faced with contradictory imperatives.

To use a metaphor, a wait in the doctor's surgery leafing through the magazines on offer, tells us that we are inadequate unless our garden is perfect, our house decorated in the latest fashion, our furnishings selected from the best stores and local artists, our record collection including only the most talked about composers and musicians, our reading list featuring only prize-winning novels, our clothes reflecting the latest trends (and the best materials) and our cuisine consisting of the best dishes prepared from ingredients bought fresh every day.

This is silly. No one can be perfect at everything any more than we can be at

---

[1] As far as I can tell, there is no film in which anyone actually said this, but John Wayne and Charlton Heston came close.

the same time a brave and dominant warrior, a high-minded Athenian citizen, a religious hermit, a pioneer, a go-ahead businessman, an excellent wife of a loving husband, a man in touch with his feminine side, an independent career woman, a dedicated mother, a philanthropic Victorian *paterfamilias*, or a fish riding a bicycle.

Clint Eastwood's Preacher in *Pale Rider* has six bullet wounds in his back and shoots down a dozen or so men in the finale. The only response that Megan receives to her shouted love for him are the echoes of her voice in the canyon. The Preacher demonstrates no virtues of forgiveness, domesticity, philanthropy, respectability, high-mindedness or entrepreneurial behaviour. How could he? The context of the film is the lawlessness of a no doubt mythical[1] Wild West in which the weak can be protected only by someone whose values are the exact opposite of theirs.

A context for today

Now we come to the nub of the matter. To decide what excellences are important today requires that we identify how we can *live respected and die regretted;* that we can identify the *purpose-to-life* for today. The apparent arbitrariness of moral decision-making, the way in which we cannot resolve moral disagreements, and the fact that we have so many contradictory demands, imply that there is no dominant view in our society and hence no list of excellences that we all share. Unlike in many earlier societies, we have no common rules for *living respected &c.*

As a result, moral relativity arises and we have come to live in an amoral world, a view that our analysis of *the end of decency* may be taken to support. Jonathan Sacks expresses something similar when he writes:

> It is often assumed that we have moved beyond morality, that instead of thinking in terms of shared, objective values we now make choices on the basis of subjective inclination. The decisions we make have, and are meant to have, validity for us alone.

---

[1] See David West *The Devil, the Goat and the Freemason - a study in the history of ideas*, Hamilton House, 2013. Dodge City was a railhead for the cattle business from 1876. With gunfighters, brothels, saloons and even bullfights, the city flourished for just ten hard-living years until the cattle business moved on.

We would not seek to impose them on others, and we resent it if others try to share their values with us. The old ideas, that there are moral rules and moral knowledge, that there are virtues we need to learn, have gone, never to return. That, at any rate, is the prevailing orthodoxy, reiterated daily in the media. [1]

The failure of moral traditions

Sacks seeks an answer in the Judaic-Christian tradition but such a tradition can provide a *purpose-to-life* only for those increasingly few people who accept a Judaic-Christian deity. As a context in common, that tradition is exhausted, and it is MacIntyre's view that all other available contexts have also been exhausted. The (moral) assumptions made not only by the Judaic-Christian tradition, but also by liberalism, capitalism and Marxism/socialism, no longer hold.

For our purposes, **Liberalism** may be represented by the views of Thomas Hobbes who justified the rule of law by reference to a social contract, whereby everyone agrees to avoid those behaviours which would damage society. The contract would be silent on all other behaviours, which is why I use Hobbes as a liberal for now. Such a contract implies the virtue of trust. If I abide by the rules of the social contract, I have to trust that you will not seek an advantage but will abide by them too.

So many people now abuse the trust of others that the excellences of liberalism – *open-mindedness, respect for the law, personal responsibility* and *consideration for others* – can no longer provide a common moral basis. In place of open-mindedness we find fundamentalism, in place of consideration we find greed and in place of responsibility we find selfishness. As Mikhail Gorbachev wrote:

A serious threat is hovering over European Culture … one can only wonder that a deep, profoundly intelligent and inherently humane … culture is retreating to the background before the primitive revelry of violence and pornography and the flood of cheap feelings and low thoughts. [2]

---

[1] Sacks, Jonathan, *The Politics of Hope*, Random House, 1997.
[2] *Perestroika: New Thinking for Our Country and the World*, Collins, 1987.

If **Capitalism** is to work, we require fair competition within the rules, including the rules of decency,[1] otherwise there is a race to the bottom. The successive crises in capitalism indicate that the race has now reached what we may hope is, but is probably not, its nadir. Competition now requires constant and expensive policing beyond the level governments are able or willing to provide. Immorality and illegality have all but become the norm. The audit process for identifying and reporting failures of governance is itself under stress and that those charged with oversight have frequently proved themselves unworthy. Rather than welcoming the stimulus of competition, business now pursues monopoly. Lying is normal. The virtues that enable capitalism to work – *fair competition, honesty, playing by the rule*s – have become unusable.

Marxism was a reaction to the conditions of the poor in the nineteenth century and was essentially optimistic, as is its close relative, **Socialism** (which one might think of as Marxism without the theory.) Socialism has had its successes. In the UK, governments from Churchill to Callaghan agreed on many socialist essentials; Cuba has a splendid health system; Chile has recovered from the CIA-inspired dictatorship of Pinochet to become a stable social democracy, and the co-determination process of industrial management in modern Germany has strong socialist roots. Sweden has long been a successful egalitarian democracy.

However, socialism was severely damaged in the monetarist years. Its virtues – *mutual concern, fraternity, sharing, help for the underdog, fairness* – have become seen as weaknesses in the face of the false icons of low taxation and trickle down, the rise of populism and attacks on the welfare system. The argument of the undeserving poor has once again raised its ugly head.

---

[1] *... if, on entering the butchers shop as a habitual customer I find him collapsing from a heart attack, and I merely remark, 'Ah! Not in a position to sell me meat today, I see,' and proceed immediately to his competitor's store to complete my purchase, I will have obviously and grossly damaged my whole relationship to him, including my economic relationship, although have done nothing contrary to the norms of the market ... Market relationships can only be sustained by being embedded in certain types of local non-market relationship, relationships of uncalculated giving and receiving ...* MacIntyre, *Dependent Rational Animals*, Carus Publishing, 1999.

Sacks writes:

> *Relationships, whether at work or in private life, become a choice between manipulating and being manipulated, exploiting or being exploited. The idea that one might value another person or an institution sufficiently to make a long-term binding commitment … begins to seem old-fashioned and naive … no relationship so intimate, no secret so private, that it cannot be confessed in front of television cameras or sold for money to the press … hard today to find a code of honour that cannot be broken for profit …* [1]

And it is MacIntyre's conclusion that:

> *The tradition of the virtues is at variance with central features of the modern economic order and more especially its individualism, its acquisitiveness and its elevation of the values of the market to a central social place* [2] *… it now becomes clear that [the tradition of the virtues] also involves a rejection of the modern political order.* [3]

If MacIntyre is right, as a society we can no longer agree on the purpose-to-life, and so have no common values and no basis for a shared moral life. Let us try an experiment. Put the following list into rank order: firstly in terms of success, and secondly in terms of virtue.

1. *The film star who marries a prince.*
2. *The cleaning lady who gives everyone a smile.*
3. *The agent who successfully deceives the enemy.*
4. *The man who gives away all his money to become a monk.*
5. *The female chieftain who defies the invader.*
6. *The soldier king who creates an empire.*
7. *The martyr, dying for his faith.*
8. *The uneducated man who retires rich at 40.*
9. *The pearly king who collects for charity, rain or shine.*
10. *The wealthy woman known for her support of the arts and her great parties.*

Homer, Skallagrimsson, Aristotle and Ignatius would each have used

---

[1] *Op. cit.*

[2] MacIntyre, *After Virtue.*

[3] *Ibid.*

different criteria and reached a different rank order, but their lists would be the same whether they used *success* or *virtue* as a criterion. For them, the successful life would have exemplified the virtues, and the virtuous life would have been successful.

Does your first list differ from your second? I would hazard a guess that it does. For many people success and virtue are at opposite poles of a continuum: the more successful, the less virtuous and vice versa. Ask a friend to try the experiment. I would guess that your and their lists will differ. Try reaching an agreement. You mind find that hard.

Our challenge

Society is increasingly psychopathic with no ability or indeed desire to live the moral life. MacIntyre declares that a new dark age is upon us, comparing our situation with the end of the Roman Empire when the barbarians gathered and Roman life became impossible. As Lyman Andrews wrote:

> *In ninth century Britain the*
> *Saxons built wooden towns, refused*
> *To enter the crumbling Roman city,*
> *Drafty and full of spirits, because*
> *The Saxons could not understand*
> *How to make the Roman heating work: so*
> *They shivered under the ruined gaze of marble.*[1]

As society fell apart, the only hope lay in groups of people seeking to maintain ways of living together. MacIntyre says of today:

> *... if the tradition of the virtues was able to survive the horrors of the last dark ages, we are not entirely without grounds for hope.*

But he then cuts the ground from under such optimism by saying:

> *This time however the Barbarians are not waiting beyond the frontiers; they have already been governing us for some time.*

---

[1] 'Lampedusa', *Fugitive Visions*, White Rabbit, 1962.

Politics has ceased to deal in ideals. Cynicism reigns. Truth has become trickery. Kind behaviour is seen as weakness. There is little support for honesty; little applause for the unselfish. It is as if morality has become counter-cultural.

> *What matters at this stage is the construction of local forms of community within which civility and the intellectual and moral life can be sustained through the new dark ages which are already upon us.*

... as MacIntyre concludes. Within our society, morality is retreating and can only be preserved by a community of people of who accept common ideals, and work together in fraternity and concord. Members will support each other in their intention to live the moral life, just as members of Alcoholics Anonymous help each other to remain sober.

Here then is our greatest challenge and opportunity: to take on the duty of sustaining civility and the moral life through the new dark ages. Our order can become one of MacIntyre's *local forms of community* in which the moral life can be continued, combatting *the horrors of the modern dark age*. As such our order is supremely important. Our order is a context within which virtues find traction. Sustaining *civility and the intellectual and moral life* must become our reason for existence. In achieving it, we shall save ourselves.

Choosing to be a freemason

St Benedict

Alasdair MacIntyre writes that society is waiting not for some new *Godot* – not for an external and mythical agency to come to our aid – but *for another, doubtless very different, St Benedict*. Set down in about 530 CE, the *Rule of St Benedict* was written to govern monastic communities voluntarily bound to live together, adopting specific virtues and agreeing to a series of *oughts*. Parts of the rule bear close similarity with freemasonry.

> *Distinctions between the brethren may be made only on merit.*
>
> *A council of all brethren will discuss and decide on matters of importance.*
>
> *Decisions of the council and Abbot* (WM?) *should be cheerfully obeyed.*
>
> *Precedence is decided by date of admission, merit or decision by the Abbot.*
>
> *Moderation is necessary in all behaviour and speech.*
>
> *The importance of divine offices* (the ritual?) *is emphasised.*
>
> *Brethren are exhorted to zeal and fraternal charity.*
>
> *Guests are to be received with courtesy.*
>
> *Clothing is to be plain and suited to the climate.*

And one that should be in freemasonry but has been driven out by PR:

> *A wayward brother who has left the monastery must be received again.*

Hammer reminds us that:

> *Masonry is and was always intended to be an initiatory organisation that an individual must seek to join. He does so not out of necessity or hope of material benefits, but out of an inner calling to greater wisdom, i.e. intellectual and spiritual light. Then after he makes that choice, he must in turn be chosen by others who agree to admit him into their assemblies.*[1]

Choosing to adopt a set of criteria is an authentic decision if the implications of the choice are explained, recognised and willingly accepted. The monks who adopted the Rule of St Benedict, chose to be governed by a set of rules,

---

[1] *Op. cit.*

after long consideration. In doing so, they committed themselves to the observance of some behaviours and the rejection of others. The rule provided the basis upon which they made their decisions thereafter.

On a parallel with the Rule of St Benedict, a man may choose to be a freemason and thus commit himself to excellences by which to live a life. Like candidates for the order of St Benedict, every potential initiate for freemasonry must understand that to become a freemason is to agree to seek to attain those excellences. Thus, freemasonry sustains a context for a purpose-to-life in exactly the same way as Aristotle's context of Athens or St Ignatius's context of early Christianity.

Choosing to be

To be clear at this point, I am not saying that everyone in the world ought to exhibit the excellences of brotherly love, relief and truth. Indeed, it should be obvious by now that there is no sense in which such a statement can be made. The moral life is not independent of human life but changes with the context in which we live.[1] It is only as conscious, evaluative beings that we give life meaning and attribute value. We, as freemasons, might be of the opinion that global society would be better if everyone did exemplify brotherly love, relief and truth, but this is a contingent statement (which may be true or false) and not a moral one.

What I am saying is that *if* a man *chooses* to be a freemason, *then* he *ought* to exhibit certain excellences of character. (The emphasis indicates the words carrying the ethical message.) The *ought* is derived from the *choice*. To be a freemason is (at least) to exemplify brotherly love, relief and truth. There is no sense in which a man can say *I want to be a freemason but not a good one* because freemasonry is a moral practice. It offers a purpose-to-life. (It might be worth your while to read that again.)

---

[1] In his *Philosophical Investigations*, (Basil Blackwell, 1967) Wittgenstein said that *sprachspiele* exist within *forms of life*. What is said and done can only be understood by reference to a form of life and a form of life is always an interpersonal or societal affair. The argument here is similar to Wittgenstein's argument against a private language. I will not go into this now. Suffice to say that the veracity of any moral judgement, which itself can only exist within a form of life, requires that it can be checked by another member of that form of life. In this way, moral judgements obey something like the verification principle in Logical Positivism.

There is no obligation on any man to choose our *peculiar system of morality veiled in allegory and illustrated by symbols.* It is a free choice and one that must be made carefully. As the Royal Arch ritual says of the candidate, *may he not enter our Order lightly, nor recede from it hastily, but pursue it steadfastly.* In making the choice to become a freemason, one accepts the obligation to adopt our excellences and principles – and this is the point in becoming a freemason. To adopt the ethical structure of freemasonry is to become a freemason, and to become a freemason is to adopt that structure. There is no meaning to the statement that one can be a freemason and not adopt our ethical structure. It would be like saying *I am a democrat but do not believe in voting.* [1]

The candidate

Chapter 58 of the Rule of St Benedict, governing applications to join the order, is worth examining. It has similarities to what our practice ought to be.

> *[Suppose] someone comes … knocking at the door, and if at the end of four or five days he has shown himself patient … and has persisted in his request, then he should be allowed to enter and stay in the guest quarters for a few days. After that, he should live … where the novices study, eat and sleep. A senior chosen for his skill should be appointed to look after them … [He] should be clearly told all the hardships and difficulties … If he promises perseverance … then after two months have elapsed let this rule be read straight through to him, and let him be told: 'This is the law under which you are choosing to serve. If you can keep it, come in. If not, feel free to leave.' If he still stands firm, he is to be taken back … and again thoroughly tested in all patience. After six months have passed, the rule is to be read to him [again], so that he may know what he is entering. If once more he stands firm, let four months go by, and then read this rule to him [yet] again. If after due reflection he promises to observe everything and to obey every command … let him then be received into the community. But he must be well aware that … from this day he is no longer free to leave the monastery, nor to shake from his neck the yoke of the rule …*

It is supremely important that a candidate for freemasonry should recognise that in joining he is choosing to enter a fraternity which lives by certain

---

[1] If a man joins the order and then acts in ways incompatible with the required excellences, this fact much be brought to his attention by the brethren. He must reform or leave. This is not just a matter of criminal behaviour.

principles. Any candidate should be clear about the need for his commitment to the specific virtues and excellences required to be a good freemason, and that the intention to become a good freemason should be his primary reason for joining. This should be explained to the candidate before he joins and continually reinforced during the period leading up to his being raised to the sublime degree of a Master Mason.[1]

Our purpose in summary

Our purpose, then, is to be a community in which the moral life can be continued, even as the virtues and virtue are lost elsewhere. Part of our work of preservation is the maintenance of the ability to trust and to be trustworthy, to be a reservoir of social capital. More importantly, we are to be a moral stronghold, combatting MacIntyre's *horrors of the modern dark age*, a context within which virtues find traction. This must become our reason for existence. Given the absence of any other agreed social or political context (an absence that neither Plato nor Aristotle would have understood) or of any widespread religious belief (which St Ignatius would have found incomprehensible), freemasonry becomes, uniquely, a vital *form of community within which civility and the intellectual and moral life can be sustained.* It is easy to view such a task as beyond us but it may be of some comfort to recognise that the task has fallen on others before.

Attacks on values happen in cycles; there are periodic intervals in human experience when scientific, religious and economic events demand new ways of understanding our relationships with others. During such upheavals moral relativity seeks to take over. One of those periods occurred in the 1800s, a period that saw freemasonry's near terminal decline. I quoted from Thomas Carlyle who railed against the destruction of virtues like expertise, imagination and devotion, as skilled handcraft was overtaken by the production line.

---

[1] No man will understand the whole body of masonic excellences right away and a candidate cannot truly make that choice until he fully understands the excellences demanded of him. Thus, the time spent as an Entered Apprentice should be seen as a time of reflection and qualification. One might well argue that no joining fee should be payable until a brother has taken his third degree, for only then will he be fully able to make a decision to join us, abide by our principles and live his life according to the virtues of the order.

On every hand, the living artisan is driven from his workshop, to make room for a speedier, inanimate one … men have lost their belief in the Invisible, and believe, and hope, and work only in the Visible … Only the material, the immediately practical, not the divine and spiritual, is important to us… Our true Deity is Mechanism.[1]

The Victorian middle class that followed managed to create a virtuous capitalism, in which decency combined with creativity and energy to bring about Britain's economic leadership in the known world. Virtuous capitalism has now been destroyed and with it the values which the middle class sustained. The barbarian attacks on decency must be resisted once again. It seems that now it is our turn.

Examples of periods of moral uncertainty, other than today and the end of the Roman Empire, include:

(1) The *Crisis of the Late Middle Ages*, uprisings all over Europe caused by a widening gap between rich and poor, increased poverty and the onset of the Little Ice Age which resulted in the great famine of 1315-17. The 100 Years War began in 1337 and the Black Death, which halved the population, ten years later. The effect was religious upheaval in which John Wyclif and the Lollards argued that as god had already chosen those to be saved, the Church was unnecessary.

(2) The *Enlightenment*, whose effect on religious belief I discussed in my book, *Deism*. One might say that before Descartes and Locke the discussion was about which form of worship was best. After them, it was largely about whether there was a god at all.

---

[1] 'A Mechanical Age' in the *Edinburgh Review*, 1829. The words could be applied to today. In *The Burnout Society* (Stanford University Press, 2015) Byung-Chul Han writes that life, *stripped of all transcendent value, has been reduced to the immanency of vital functions*; in his *Burnout Society*, Stanford Univ. Press, 2015.

The virtues of freemasonry

Here is a lovely charge from the Dumfries No. 4 MS of 1710:

> *[E]very man yt is a massone or enters y^r inters y^r interest to aggrandise & satisfie his curiositie looke to ye following charge if any of ye be guilty of ye following Immoralitys see yt you Repent & amend speedily for you will find it a hard thing to fall into ye hands [of] our angry god and more especialy you yt are under the voues take hee[d] yt you keep ye ath and promise you made in the presence of allmighty god think not yt a mental Reservation or Equivocation will serve for to be sure eury word you speak the whole time of your Admission is ane oath and god will examin you according to the purness of your heart and cleaness of your hands it is ane sharp edged tool yt you are playing with beware you cut not your fingers we intreat you that ye forfit not your Saluation for any other seeming content.*

My transliteration of this runs:

> *Every mason, or anyone who enters the order to gain power and influence or to satisfy his curiosity, should take notice of the following charge. If any of you are guilty of these sins, see to it that you repent and make good without delay, for you will find it hard to fall into the hands of an angry God. You are still under your vows, so be careful to maintain the oath and promise you made in the presence of that God. Do not think that mental reservation or equivocation will serve because every word you spoke during the whole of your admission into freemasonry constitutes an oath and God will examine you according to the purity of your heart and cleanliness of your hands. It is a sharp-edged tool that you are playing with, so beware of cutting your fingers. We entreat you not to forfeit your salvation for any apparent pleasure.*

(In the following pages, I will generally modernise spelling and grammar in quotes.)

The modern charge after the initiation claims at one point that freemasonry practises every moral and social virtue. As we have seen, virtues and excellences from differing contexts will contradict each other and thus such a claim borders on nonsense. As difficult as it may be, we must at least make a stab at what excellences freemasonry genuinely values.

The three grand principles, one might assume, have been in the forefront of the minds of masons from time immemorial although the phrase *brotherly love, relief and truth* itself seems not to appear before Preston in 1772.

Understanding brotherly love

The phrase *brotherly love* makes its first appearance in Anderson's 1723 *Constitutions*, where it is described as *the foundation and capstone, the cement and glory of this ancient fraternity*, but the sentiments appear much earlier. Around 1420 the *Regius Poem* reads:

> … *each one shall teach the other, and love together as sister and brother … Masons should never one another call, within the craft amongst them all, neither subject nor servant, my dear brother, though he be not so perfect as is another, each shall call other fellows by friendship …*

A similar charge appears in the Cooke MS of about 1450:

> … *that ye love together as ye were brethren, and hold together truly; and he that hath most cunning [skill] teach it to his fellow.*

and the Dowland MS of about 1500:

> *That they should be true each of them to other, and that they should love truly together.*

In 1714 the Kevan MS introduces a greeting we are used to, *Brother John, greet you well* with a reply, *God's good greeting to you, dear brother.*

The five points are among the oldest examples of moral teaching that we have. To live by the undertakings of the five points of fellowship is to be trustworthy; to act upon them is to trust. They seem to have been more important in earlier times. Since there was initially just the one degree, the five points were not tucked away in the third, as they are today. They appear in just about all exposures, with slight variations. To choose just one example, the Chetwode Crawley MS *c.*1720 runs:

> *How many points of fellowship are there?*
> *Five: foot to foot, knee to knee, heart to heart, hand to hand, ear to ear.*

In this MS, the five points are followed by both the (modern) first and second degree words and so it could be argued that they belong in the first degree. An explanation of them is provided in the 1760 *Three Distinct Knocks*:

Hand to hand	*I always will put forth my hand to serve a brother as far as lies in my power.*
Foot to Foot	*I will never be afraid to go a foot out of my way to serve a brother.*
Knee to knee	*When I kneel down to prayers I will never forget to pray for my brother as well as myself.*
Breast to Breast	*I will keep my brother's secrets as my own.*
Left-hand supporting the back	*I will always be willing to support a brother as far as lies in my power.*

Note the use of the phrase *as far as lies in my power.* A 1725 version similarly states *as far as your ability will allow you.*[1] Both are perhaps better than today's somewhat mealy-mouthed *without being detrimental to myself or family.*

A more personal relationship

In discussion, Glyn Jarrett reminded me of C.S. Lewis on love,[2] and in particular Lewis's comments on the Greek φιλία (*philia*), true friendship. Lewis writes that to the Greeks, such friendship seemed *the happiest and most fully human of all loves; the crown of life and the school of virtue.* The tragedy of the modern world, Lewis writes, is that it seems to ignore *philia*, which is a form of love central to masonry. The five points of fellowship indicate a personal relationship between masonic brothers. The *Long Closing* reads in part:

> *Let me impress upon your minds, and may it be instilled into your hearts, that every human creature has a just claim on your kind offices. I therefore trust that you will be good to all. More particularly do I recommend to your care the household of the faithful.*

The *household of the faithful* is perhaps the community of freemasons joined in *philia* with a commitment to the order and its obligations. *Be good to everyone, but love your brother* is the original statement of virtue in freemasonry.

Understanding relief

Here is a thought for you:

---

[1] *Institutions of Freemasonry,* 1725.

[2] C.S. Lewis, *The Four Loves*, Geoffrey Bles, 1960.

Though I speak with the tongues of men and of angels, and have not charity, I am become as sounding brass, or a tinkling cymbal.

Compare this with:

If I speak in the tongues of men or of angels, but do not have love, I am only a resounding gong or a clanging cymbal.

Both are 1 *Corinthians* 13, the first passage from the King James and the second from the New International version of the Bible. The difference rests on their translation of the Greek word αγαπη (*agape*). The *Catholic Encyclopaedia*, my regular resource on such matters, reads:

… charity is that habit or power which disposes us to love God above all creatures for Himself, and to love ourselves and out neighbours for the sake of god.

So the religious sense of the word *charity* is an act of love – *the love of God for man and of man for God* – and only an act carried out for love is considered an act of charity. Today the word *charity* has today come to mean little more than giving money to an impersonal if worthy cause, for which the word *philanthropy* is suitable.

Philanthropy is not the meaning of the word *relief* either. The target of relief is a known (and loved) person, as in the modern *relieve and befriend with unhesitating cordiality every brother who might need your assistance.* Whenever it appears in earlier documents, the word *relief* is used in connection with improvident masons. The lodge box, found particularly in early Scottish lodges, speaks to this:

Every new brother at his making is … to deposit something for the relief of indigent and decay'd Brethren, as the Candidate shall think fit to bestow …[1]

Relief is not just about money but also about action and emotion: visiting people when they are sick, comforting people, acting from the heart. Dumfries No 4 implies that the recipient is known to the mason:

Visit the sick; comfort and pray for them and let them not be in any distress that is in your power to prevent. If god calls them hence, attend their funeral. [Be] affable and

---

[1] Anderson's *Constitutions*. *Indigent* means *poor*. *Decayed* means something like *handicapped by age*.

kind to everyone but more especially to widows and the fatherless. Stand stoutly on their behalf, defend their interests and relieve their necessities …[1]

In lodge we collect *alms*, yet another word associated with relief.[2] The word *alms* derives from the Greek ἔλεος (*eleos*) meaning mercy or compassion. Its early meaning is relief of the poor as a religious duty. Giving money without mercy or compassion is not relief. The initiate is told that among the many

Geo Oliver DD

under our banner there are those *who from circumstances of unforeseen calamity and misfortune are reduced to the lowest ebb of poverty and distress;* that it is on their behalf that *we awaken the feelings of every newly made brother.* Dr George Oliver *(left)* adds:

Wherever a mason may stray … he will always find a home; he will always meet with some kind friend and Brother to give him welcome, to greet him with the right hand of fellowship, to promote his interests, and to give him comfort and consolation in his distress.

I think that it is fair to say that we have been scared off the practice of relief by accusations that freemasons look after their own. Our response to such accusation should have been to say, *Of course we do!* but in fact we have responded defensively and advertised our philanthropy towards non-masonic causes.[3]

There is clearly nothing wrong with philanthropy, but it is not the centre of

---

[1] The Dumfries MS argues that the Mason should especially concern himself with widows and orphans even though, in a curious phrase, *this bread be thrown upon uncertain waters.*

[2] The word *alimony* is connected.

3 As the United Grand Lodge of England did with their press release, *Enough is enough.*

masonic life. Patrick Byrne, like many masons, longs for a return to the old ways of charitable giving:

> *I am one of those traditional masons who miss the old days, when we did our bit for charity and basked in the knowledge that no one else knew what we had done. I know that we began to publicise our charitable work as a response to those who wished to denigrate our order, but I'm not sure that in making our charitable works public, we have accrued any benefit.* [1]

The use of charitable donations for purely PR purposes has, of course, no place in masonry.

Given the issues that society faces today, and will face even more tomorrow, the virtue of relief is more important than ever, and lodges ought to be persuaded to put more money aside to provide help in the future for their own brethren and widows in distress.

Understanding truth

Of the three grand principles, truth is the most difficult to describe. In my book *The Goat, the Devil and the Freemason* I wrote, all too hastily, that truth concerns honesty in word and deed. A reviewer took me to task about that, clearly wanting the word *truth* to have some spiritual or religious meaning. I really do not think it does, but I do agree that it means more than I said.

It is difficult to find what we might call a capital-T use of the word before Preston, and I am not sure that Preston knew what he was talking about when he wrote:

> *By this principle we are taught to secure the favourable opinions of the world by the sincerity of our conduct. It is a divine attribute and the foundation of every virtue; while to the former principles it adds energy and effect. How is this principle applied in masonry? In masonry this principle has peculiar influence, for swayed by it in the Lodge, hypocrisy and deceit are unknown, sincerity and plain dealing mark our conduct, and heart and tongue combine to promote the welfare, and rejoice at the prosperity of our brethren.*

… much of which sounds suspiciously like waffle.

---

[1] Byrne, Patrick, *The membership crisis in Freemasonry*, hinchley-wood-lodge.com.

In the English language, the word *true* takes on a range of meanings. We speak of a true friend, a true emotion, the true path, the true heir and true north. We speak of a mechanical fitting being true, an archer aiming true, of remaining true to one's beliefs and of a portrait being a true likeness. The *Regius* poem uses the word in the sense of factual truth, saying that geometry is a discipline that distinguishes truth (accuracy) from falsehood (inaccuracy).

> *Gemetré the seventh syens hyt ysse,*
> *That con deperte falshed from trewthe y-wys.*

The word appears, significantly after the five points of fellowship, in the 1696 Edinburgh Register House MS where the instruction appears, *shake hands and you will be acknowledged a true* (in the sense of genuine) *mason*. The exposure *Shibboleth* describes masons as *true to each other*, meaning loyal as I take it. In the early rituals, a true mason is characterised by such words as loyal, unfeigning and genuine, as in true to our principles, a true and constant friend whose love of his brethren is truly demonstrated. Here, it seems, is the meaning of *truth* in the three grand principles, the statement of which might be better punctuated *brotherly love: relief and truth* (note colon). Relief and truth are nothing more, and nothing less, than ways of showing love. We demonstrate our love by helping a brother and by being faithful and loyal to him.

The four cardinal[1] virtues

The quartet of prudence, fortitude, temperance and justice appears in the charge after initiation, *Let prudence direct you, temperance chasten you, fortitude support you and justice be the guide of all your actions.* Dr Roy Murray argues[2] that these cardinal virtues have been connected with masonry since time immemorial but while they adorn the four corners of the Grand Temple in Freemasons' Hall in London, I have not found them in rituals before Preston. Nevertheless they appear in the semi-canonical *Wisdom of Solomon*, from about 200 BCE:[3]

> *And if a man love righteousness, her labours are virtues: for she teacheth temperance and*

---

[1] *Cardinal* is from the Latin *cardo*, meaning hinge as in the hinge of a door.
[2] Roy Murray, 'The four cardinal virtues and the tassels in the lodge room', *AQC*, Vol. 107, 1999.
[3] Jews & Protestants don't consider the book canonical but Catholics & Orthodox believers do.

prudence, justice and fortitude: which are such things as men can have nothing more profitable in their life.

In the *Compendium of the Catechism of the Catholic Church*,[1] the *principal human virtues* are described as the:

> *... habitual and stable perfections of the intellect and will that govern our actions, order our passions and guide our conduct according to reason and faith. They are acquired and strengthened by the repetition of morally good acts and they are purified and elevated by divine grace.*

The *Compendium* says of them:[2]

> Prudence *disposes reason to discern in every circumstance our true good and to choose the right means for achieving it.*
>
> Justice *consists in the firm and constant will to give to others their due.*
>
> Fortitude *assures firmness in difficulties and constancy in the pursuit of the good. It reaches even to the ability of possibly sacrificing one's own life for a just cause.*
>
> Temperance *moderates the attraction of pleasures, assures the mastery of the will over instincts and provides balance in the use of created goods.*

Prudence

The classical authors thought of prudence as the ability to tell right from wrong, consulting others and seeking advice, as well as the skill of speaking without giving offence. When the ritual says *Let prudence direct you*, it is not telling us to avoid risk, but to put thought into finding the right thing to do, using care when announcing a decision and giving advice to others.

Fortitude

Plato thought of this as the soldier's virtue but for Aquinas it is that virtue which gives us the strength to do what should be done; enabling us to overcome fear, remaining steady in pursuit of the good. The *beserkers*, those Norse warriors so admired in the sagas, who fought in an enraged and probably drug-induced trance would not have been admired by Aristotle, for

---

[1] *Libreria Editrice Vaticana*, 2005.

[2] *Compendium*, part three, questions 380 to 383, lightly edited.

whom fortitude is facing known odds rationally and accepting death only as necessary to the defence of what is right. For us, fortitude is about maintaining our principles in the face *the attacks of the insidious*, and those temptations and persuasions that stealthily, deceitfully and treacherously beguile us into unworthy actions.

Temperance

Plato sees temperance as a matter of harmony, avoiding excess. In his commentary on Aristotle, Aquinas writes:

> *The temperate man desires whatever pleasures are useful to the health and well-being of the body, and he wants them according to right measure and as he ought. He desires other pleasures only if they are not a hindrance to health, nor opposed to what is honourable, nor beyond his means.* [1]

For Aquinas, temperance is about the absence of (improper) desire; for St Paul it is about controlling improper desire.[2] This distinction matters, I think, and Aristotle makes use of it when distinguishing between the *temperate* and the *continent* man:

> *Whereas the temperate man is equable by nature so that he does not experience strong desires, the continent man is of a more energetic nature and therefore does experience such desires, yet governs them according to the dictates of reason ...*[3]

It is in the sense of *continence* that the common gavel *denotes the force of conscience which should keep down all vain and unbecoming thoughts*. It is continence (controlling our desires), rather than temperance (not having desires), that seems descriptive of the masonic life. As the 1730 pamphlet *A Defence of Masonry* says, the design of freemasonry is *to subdue our passions*.[4]

On the other hand, the Long Working Tools of the Second Degree instructs us to make our *passions and prejudices coincide with the strict line of duty*, which is more like Aristotle's temperance, achieving the state of desiring only our

---

[1] *Commentary on the Nicomachean Ethics*, trnsl. C.I. Litzinger OP, Henry Regnery Co., 1964.
[2] For example see 1 *Corinthians* 7.
[3] *Nicomachean Ethics*, Penguin Classics, new Edition 2004.
[4] Douglas Knoop *et al.*, *The Early Masonic Catechisms*, *Quatuor Coronati* Lodge, 1943, 1975.

duty. Perhaps this is another journey from the rough to the smooth ashlar, one from continence to temperance, a journey doubtless assisted by age as the blood of youth cools.

Justice

Isaiah 28:17 makes justice sound peculiarly masonic, *I will make justice the measuring line and righteousness the plumb line.* Aristotle's view of justice is similar to the Senior Warden's duty to see that every brother has his due. What is due, says Aristotle, depends upon merit, just desserts as we might say. Aristotle's vice of *pleonexia* (greed) is seeking more than one's due, a vice Ivan Boesky celebrated.

The problem we face in our society is that we have no view in common of what constitutes just desserts; no common view of fairness or equity. Michael Sandel writes:

> *To ask whether a society is just is to ask how it distributes the things we prize – income and wealth, duties and rights, powers and opportunities, offices and honours. A just society distributes these goods in the right way; it gives each person his or her due ... The hard questions begin when we are asked what people are due and why.*[1]

The free market capitalist would argue that his investment, skills, knowledge and risk-taking justify a greater share of the world's goods. Most social democracies temper capitalism with a concern for the disadvantaged, through a welfare system or positive discrimination. Communism requires state control over all goods and services, distributing them according to perceived need. Sandel again writes:

> *Justice is inescapably judgemental ... questions of justice are bound up with the competing notions of honour and virtue, pride and recognition. Justice is not only about the right way to distribute things. It is also about the right way to value things.*

However, there is a procedural sense in which justice is about impartiality; making decisions *without* fear or favour; *not* being swayed by popular opinion;

---

[1] *Justice*, Allen Lane, 2009.

not taking bribes; consulting with others to see all sides of the issue,[1] but for freemasons impartiality is only a part of what we mean by justice. We have a moral core,[2] values held in common which provide a basis on which we apply justice. As masons, justice calls on us to help the unhappy and needy, especially our brethren in distress.[3]

You swore with generous gifts to care
For those to sorrow bidden.[4]

The *Long Closing* reminds us of our fallibility:

Remember that at this pedestal … you have promised to remind him in the most gentle manner of his failings and to aid and vindicate his character whenever wrongfully traduced; to suggest the most candid, the most palliating and the most favourable circumstances, even when his conduct is justly liable to reprehension and blame.[5]

Justice starts with the *household of the faithful*, which I described earlier as that community of freemasons joined in brotherly love *(philia)* with a commitment to the order and its obligations. George Oliver wrote:

As we are none of us free from faults, it is the duty of every brother to bear with the infirmities, to pardon the errors, and to be kind and considerate towards those with whom he is so intimately connected … [6]

We are to take our brother's part, be on his side, do our best to help him out of his troubles, even when his conduct is *justly liable to reprehension and blame*. Being brothers, we cannot pick and choose when to take sides. Regret, apology and amends would no doubt be required, but:

---

[1] *Do not follow the crowd in doing wrong. When you give testimony in a lawsuit, do not pervert justice by siding with the crowd.* Exodus 23:2. *Do not accept a bribe, for a bribe blinds the eyes of the wise and twists the words of the innocent.* Deuteronomy 16:19. [It] *was customary for the king to consult experts in matters of law and justice ... the wise men who understood the times.* Esther 1:13.

[2] The word here is *core* and not *code*.

[3] Isaiah 1:17. *Learn to do well; seek judgment, relieve the oppressed, judge the fatherless, plead for the widow.*

[4] Walking Charge', in *St Laurence Working*.

[5] *Long Closing, loc. cit.*

[6] *The Book of the Lodge*, The Aquarian Press, 1986.

You swore to deal in honesty
With each true heart around you;
That honour bright should ever be
T'unbroken bond twixt him and thee;
Nor wrong, nor guile, nor cruel fraud
Should loose or break that holy cord
With which these vows have bound you.[1]

For a freemason, a just decision is one which we have tested for impartiality by consulting others, that is made without fear of popular opinion; that seeks no personal reward, and is in tune with our principles, mindful of our vows concerning brotherly love and mercy, the *unbroken bond*.

Patriotism and godliness

Virtues and excellences change over time.[2] The virtues of patriotism and godliness are described in less and less specific terms as time goes by. The Dumfries No. 4 MS, from about 1710, says of patriotism:

You shall be true to the lawful King of the Realm and pray for his safety ... be no partaker of any treasonable designs against his person and government.

It positions the person of the king as the focus of patriotism, written as it was during the period of the Jacobite rebellions: the time of James II landing at Kinsale in 1685, Bonnie Dundee (1689), the Battle of the Boyne (1690), and James Francis Edward Stuart, the Old Pretender in 1715.

Dumfries was concerned in a very personal way. As a city in the Borders, it was uncomfortable placed between the English Protestant Hanoverian crown and the Scottish Catholic Jacobite rebels, but the Old Pretender's landing in 1716 at Peterhead, a long way from Dumfries, was rendered irrelevant by the earlier defeat of the Jacobite forces, and the statement started to soften. By 1723, the focus of patriotism had changed from King to nation.

---

[1] 'Walking Charge', *op. cit.* Not early ritual, dating from 1947, but neatly encompassing ideas.

[2] It is amusing to think that our forebears thought it necessary to remind us not to argue in lodge, not *to drink drunk*, not to play cards for money, and not to swear or use obscene gestures. A lovely early phrase is *taciturnity and concord*. In the eighteenth century, *taciturnity* meant *being habitually silent*, while the word *concord*, derived from the Latin, meant *hearts together*.

James II landing at Kinsale in 1685

> *A mason is a peaceable Subject to the Civil Powers … and is never to be concern'd in Plots and Conspiracies against the Peace and Welfare of the Nation … So that if a brother should be a Rebel against the State, he is not to be countenanced.*[1]

Softening further, in the same year *A Mason's Examination* says that masons should be no *perjured Plotters or Conspirators against the establish'd Government,*[2] while in 1735 Smith's *Pocket Companion* says a mason should be *a peaceable subject, conforming cheerfully to the government under which he lives.*[3]

The specificity of the charge declines as the likelihood of rebellion recedes and the Jacobite cause was finally brought to an end in 1760 with the defeat in Quiberon Bay by Sir Edward Hawkes of a Jacobite supporting French fleet. It is true that Bonnie Prince Charlie attempted a rising in 1745, spending three days in Dumfries, taking Carlisle and getting as far south as Derbyshire. With no local support, he turned back through Dumfries again,

---

[1] Anderson, *The Constitutions of the Free-Masons*, 1723.

[2] Knoop *op. cit.*

[3] *Ibid.*

much to the citizens' dismay,[1] but he was decisively defeated at Culloden, and in 1765, *Shibboleth* provides the essence of the modern version:

A mason is obliged to conform to the laws of the place in which he resides, to avoid all combination against the peace and order of governments …[2]

Pierre Brossolette

Even as weak as this is, it is still not indefeasible and Keith Doney writes of the heroism of brethren, who refused to *conform to the laws* or *avoid all combination against the peace*.[3] They included Pierre Brossolette, Martial Brigouleix, Rolf & Serge l'Hermite and Georges Lapierre who, during the 1940-44 Nazi occupation of France, did all they could to make life difficult for the Nazis and the Vichy government. Bro. Brossolette threw himself to his death from a high window, for fear that he might reveal information about the Resistance under torture. Bro. Brigouleix was shot in a group of hostages and Bro. Lapierre died in Dachau concentration camp. They were not, to their eternal credit, *peaceable subjects*.

True godliness

Religious demands may also be be in conflict with political ones. The *Antient*

---

[1] He demanded a thousand pairs of shoes by the next day. The city could only manage 255. As romantic as Charlie was, the attention of the English government at the time was directed more towards the war of Austrian Succession.

[2] A.C.F. Jackson, *English Masonic Exposures 1760–1769*, Lewis Masonic, 1986.

[3] *Freemasonry in France during the Nazi Occupation*, PhD Thesis for the University of Aston in Birmingham, May 1993, and 'French Freemasonry and the Resistance 1940–1944', *Freemasonry Today*, April 2002.

Charges and Regulations uses the term *civil magistrate*, as opposed to *ecclesiastical* authority. The nineteenth century Presbyterian Robert Lewis Dabney wrote:[1]

> … *few governments are strictly just; and the inquiry therefore arises how shall the Christian citizen act, under an oppressive command of the civil magistrate? I reply, if the act which he requires is not positively a sin per se, it must be obeyed … If the thing commanded by the civil magistrate is positively sinful, then the Christian citizen must refuse obedience, but yield submission to the penalty therefor. Who is to be the judge when the act required of the citizen … is morally wrong? I reply, the citizen himself … Every intelligent being lies under moral relations to God.*

Note the last sentence.

At the beginning of the first degree, the Chaplain expresses the hope that the candidate *may be the better enabled to unfold the beauties of true godliness,* but just as the instruction regarding patriotism has changed over time, so has the instruction regarding true godliness. The Dumfries No. 4 MS calls us to serve the true god, keep his *ten words* (the commandments), to be true and steadfast to the *holy catholic*[2] church, shun heresy and schism, and observe the sabbath. The wording alludes to the religious splits taking place around the time of the first Great Awakening, and in 1723, the mason is told to be *no innovator in religious affairs,* not to invent yet another form of Christianity! Nevertheless, by 1725 the mason is advised merely to *serve god according to the best of his knowledge,* perhaps recognising that divergence in belief was impossible to stop. Dabney's words amount to much the same.[3]

Ten years later, we get what sounds like defeatism, in the instruction that *religious disputes are never suffered in lodge* [because] *we pursue the universal religion of religion of nature.* This apparent bit of deism accepts that the number of beliefs had increased so much that the only way to maintain harmony in lodge was to ban discussion of religion altogether. By 1765, we find *Shibboleth* saying of

---

[1] *Systematic Theology,* 1878. Published online by PB ministries.

[2] From the Apostles' Creed. The word *catholic* here means *proper* not *Roman.*

[3] The Great Awakening started in New England and then spread back to the UK via John and Charles Wesley. It is usually dated to the 1730s but elements pre-date this, for example in the work of Benjamin Keach, Thomas Secker (whose portrait by Joshua Reynolds hangs in the National Portrait Gallery) and Matthew Henry.

masons that … *with respect to particular notions, modes of faith and worship and the like they are left to judge for themselves.*

What a long way from the ardour of the Dumfries MS! Today we are merely told *not to be an enthusiast, persecutor, slanderer or reviler of religion;* that we should not get over-excited about religion (*an enthusiast*), not upset believers (*a persecutor*), not make incorrect accusations (*a slanderer*) nor speak abusively of it (*reviler*). An atheist would have less trouble with this than a Jesuit.

Both patriotism and godliness are expressed in such vague terms today that neither can be thought of as virtues or excellences that define masons.

Truth, honour and virtue

The *Charge after Initiation* lists specific excellences of character to which our attention is *particularly and forcibly directed*. Some of these – secrecy, fidelity and obedience – are more or less the bylaws of our order. So let us skip these and focus on a nineteenth century addition to the ritual, the instruction to *indelibly imprint on* our hearts *the sacred dictates of Truth, of Honour, and of Virtue* – a triplet with a lovely sound but no obvious meaning.

The problem is with the capital letters. We have looked at truth and virtue, so let us now focus on the word *Honour* where, unlike the other two, we can find a capital-H use. It is a tricky word, as Falstaff implies:

> *Honour pricks me on. Yea, but how if honour prick me off when I come on? How then? Can honour set to a leg? No. Or an arm? No. Or take away the grief of a wound? No. Honour hath no skill in surgery, then? No. What is honour? A word. What is in that word 'honour'? Air. A trim reckoning. Who hath it? He that died o'Wednesday.*[1]

In *a society of men who prize honour and virtue above the external advantages of rank and fortune,* the word is in direct contrast to Boesky's praise of greed: a freemason is one who would never put material reward above the requirements of the moral life; never take a bribe; always pay his due; never take advantage of another; never accept undeserved preferment.

With a rather different implication, the *Taylor's Lectures* run: *The man of honour*

---

[1] *Henry IV Part One*: Act 5 Scene 1.

scorns to do an ill action … deeming vice as something beneath him. Here is a much grander use of the word, one worthy of a capital H. It is connected with the Aristotelian word *magnanimity*:

> *The man of true honour will not content himself with a literal discharge of his duties as a man and a citizen, but raises and dignifies them to magnanimity, giving where he might with propriety refuse, and forgiving when he might with justice resent, ever deeming it more honourable to forgive than to resent an injury.* [1]

The word used in moral philosophy is *supererogation*, going beyond what is due. Tennyson uses Sir Galahad[2] as the personification of purity. He abstained from all worldly pleasures and was resistant to all temptation:

> *My good blade carves the casques of men,*
> *My tough lance thrusteth sure,*
> *My strength is as the strength of ten,*
> *Because my heart is pure.*

and

> *I never felt the kiss of love,*
> *Nor maiden's hand in mine.*
> *More bounteous aspects on me beam,*
> *Me mightier transports move and thrill;*
> *So keep I fair thro' faith and prayer*
> *A virgin heart in work and will.*

A summary of masonic virtues

While we may enjoy the fantasy of supererogation, the reality is that we are ordinary men doing our best. It is freemasonry that helps us make that best, better, but in truth there is no capital-T, capital-V or even the capital-H that rules our lives like Sir Galahad. What we can aspire to is doing our duty, well and willingly, being true to our obligations and placing brotherly love at the forefront of every decision we make. To live by *the Five Points of Fellowship* is to be trustworthy. To act upon them is to trust. The five points indicate a personal responsibility for our masonic brethren and, while the habit of

---

[1] First lecture, seventh section.

[2] Christopher Ricks (ed.), *Tennyson: A selected edition*, Longman, 1989.

loving our brethren makes us more loving of mankind, such love was originally directed towards our brethren in freemasonry.

Brotherly love may be partly defined by the phrase *all in it together*, and being brothers, we cannot pick and choose when to take sides. The words we use are *alms*, *relief* and *charity*, not *philanthropy*. The target of relief is always an individual and, in its original meaning, relief was about helping a fellow mason. Relief may be about money but it is equally about behaviour, acting from the heart. Charity is an act of love and only an act of love is an act of charity. Giving alms is acting out of mercy and compassion. A *true* mason is unfeigning and genuine; he is true to our ideals, a true and constant friend whose love of his brethren is truly demonstrated. Being true to each other, masons set an example for society.

Let prudence direct you is an instruction to use reason and logic, to think about moral issues, and to be open to advice. It is also about choosing our words carefully. *Fortitude* is about acting for the right motives, and maintaining our principles in the face of threat or persuasion to act otherwise. *Temperance* calls us to a life managed by reason, resisting temptations while experiencing human desires and feelings. In freemasonry, a *just* action is one that is tested for impartiality, made without fear of popular opinion, unmotivated by hope of personal reward and positively consistent with our principles.

The decencies of a Victorian gentleman will generally be admired within the order. We do not expect supererogation of ourselves. We are an order of ordinary men with responsibilities and ties, doing our level best.

Practice and institution

Shortly before her death in 1943, Simone Weil *(left)* wrote *The Need for Roots* in

response to a request from the Free French government for a programme of regeneration of the country after the war. Her basic premise was that:

We must first of all choose everything which is purely and genuinely good, without the slightest consideration for expediency, applying no other test than that of genuineness ... everything which is concerned only with evil, hatred, meanness must in like manner be rejected.[1]

Her words remind us that there can be no contradiction between what we say and what we do. As a moral order, the principles we hold must be reflected in the way we act and in the way we manage.

Tinkering

In the day-to-day administration of any enterprise, small improvements can add up. Tom Peters says:

I have long observed that one of the primary distinguishing characteristics of the best leaders is their personal thirst for and continued quest for new/small/practical ideas.[2]

True as this is, the revitalisation of masonry itself is more than a matter of tinkering. None of these have been of any help in reversing our decline:[3]

---

[1] Simone Weil, *The Need for Roots*, Routledge & Kegan Paul, 1952.

[2] *Thriving on Chaos*, Macmillan, 1991.

[3] They may of course have other benefits.

- Magazines.
- Research lodges.
- Public relations.
- Education officers.
- Improvements to masonic buildings.
- Change from 'proper solicitation' to 'invitation to apply.'
- Recruitment drives using media advertisements.

Nor does it seem to matter whether meetings start early or late, are held on weekdays or Saturdays, with extravagant or simple festive boards. Nor are recruitment and retention dependent upon whether dining costs are included in lodge dues or paid separately, or whether lodges hold ceremonies with single or multiple candidates. Reflecting on such data, Maurice (Harry) Kellerman[1] commented:

Are we asking the right questions? Are we clear on what the central core of freemasonry really is? Why should we seek to preserve it? [2]

Peter Thornton has argued that it is not freemasonry that is in decline but the institution that surrounds it:

... the moral and ethical teaching [freemasonry] espouses has not altered and will always be part of a democratic, civilised society. What is in decline is the ... membership ... The distinction must be made or we will continue to advocate fixing something that is not broken. [3]

Andrew Hammer regrets that for some brethren, masonry is about:

... simple brotherhood, good times and philanthropy, and should not be bothered with contemplating anything beyond what can be easily and completely understood by all. [4]

He adds:

And here is the greatest danger facing the craft today.

---

[1] Eminent Australian educator and freemason (1902-2000). Papers of merit are referred to by the Australian Masonic Research Council as *Kellerman Lectures*.

[2] *The Challenge of Changes in Membership in New South Wales*, AMRC Conference, 1992.

[3] *Nine out of ten Freemasons would attack Moscow in Winter* AMRC Conference, 1992.

[4] *Op. cit.*

Kirk C. White writes:

> *The lessons of freemasonry are meant to be lived and not simply learned … In order for freemasonry to reach its stated goals it needs to be a daily part of each brother's life.*[1]

Perhaps most significantly, R. Pottinger advised that:

> *The task is not to impose yesterday's 'normal' on a changed today, but to change the organisation to fit the new realities … [Freemasonry] has its roots in traditionalism and conservatism set in an autocratic environment in which decisions flow down the chain to be obeyed and few real avenues exist to pass messages back through the hierarchy, and with a generally low-perceived benefit from trying. … [We] must create an environment where new and possibly radical thought is encouraged and two-way communication is considered essential. Only then can the process of renewal and renaissance start.*[2]

I find myself in agreement with all these remarks.

Engineering

I have argued that our relevance to society lies in being a community in which the moral life can be continued, even as the virtues are lost elsewhere, and that only by focusing on the meaning of freemasonry can we bring about a reverse in the trend of membership. As an analogy, consider the commercial organisation that focuses solely on profit and thereby fails. It has forgotten that profit is the reward, not the product itself. On the whole, British companies have been run by accountants and have focused on cost saving and short-term profit. The UK now has little motor industry. German management focused on engineering and BMW, Mercedes, Volkswagen and Porsche are industry leaders.

Our tinkering to date has ignored the need for engineering. Tinkering assumes that the old audience is still there and that minor adjustments can be made to attract it again – but we really must recognise that the source of candidates which sustained us for a hundred years has gone. Our challenge now is to reach a new audience, one that is unlike the middle class we have

---

[1] *Operative Freemasonry: a manual for restoring light and vitality to the fraternity*, Five Gates Publishing, 2012.
[2] 'New Zealand Freemasonry in 2005', *Transactions of Masters and Past Masters Lodge No. 130*, Christchurch, New Zealand, 1997.

been used to. More self-possessed, better educated and more egalitarian, it has a different relationship with time and is often in employment that is temporary and shifting, apt to change at short notice. Given the poor state of management in the UK today, this audience has little upward loyalty and has had enough of autocracy.

Much of what happens in the modern organisation actively disengages people and the new audience will not accept similarly bad behaviour in voluntary organisations. With the decline of job satisfaction and engagement at work, and the decline of religion in society, this new audience is actively seeking meaning and fellowship which the old middle class took for granted. Our own management practices must therefore be in tune with our professed values or this new audience will turn its back on us. Behaviour acceptable to the old middle class is not necessarily acceptable to the new audience.

Hard questions

A firm stance on *Brotherly Love, Relief and Truth* will be a welcome beacon in the darkness, but our new candidates want to see a positive message that actually guides our behaviour. Words alone will not do. Mission statements are often inconsistent with the actions of the organisation. It is vital that we show we are different. Donald Schön differentiated between *theory-in-use*, what we actually do, and *espoused theory*, what we like to believe we do.[1] For example, many company reports say that people are their greatest asset. This is *espoused theory*. Actions that cut training spend demonstrate *theory-in-use*. Organisational learning starts with surfacing theories-in-use and identifying the gap between them and espoused theory.

To become a bastion for morality, freemasonry must ensure that the protection of the moral life truly becomes our guiding spirit and that the spirit of brotherhood guides all our actions. We must promulgate a community in which every action is based on trust; where our giving is truly of alms motivated by love; and all our actions show that we are true to one another. This must be our *theory-in-use*, not just *espoused theory*.

---

[1] With Chris Argyris, *Theory in practice: Increasing professional effectiveness*, Jossey-Bass, 1974.

It is vital that we avoid defensiveness. Poor organisations hide from problems, denying their existence; good organisations embrace them. In *The Future of Management*, Gary Hamel[1] invites organisational leaders to consider some hard questions. Slightly reworded, two such questions run:

- *Can you create an organisation where the spirit of community binds people together?*
- *Can you create a sense of mission that motivates extraordinary contributions?*

To help answer these big questions, lets us start with some lesser ones. Accepting Hamel's challenge, we might ask:

Where are the biggest gaps between the rhetoric and reality in our order?

What are the values we have the hardest time living up to?

Does ego ever interfere with our ideals?

How do we resolve conflict? By reference to our principles and vision or by politics?

Is our leadership remote or approachable?

With whom do our leaders participate?

Are we genuinely open to new ideas?

Whom do we promote - those with new ideas or those who agree with us?

What do we do to discover talent throughout the order?

Internal and external goods

Not understanding what we are, people outside freemasonry are tempted to look for financial or other gains, those which MacIntyre refers to as *external goods*, things having a tangible value. People can understand external goods and in a cynical world many argue that freemasonry *must* offer these: men must join for business contacts; it must be a way to get on; there must be financial benefits. When we deny these, people are mystified and ask, *Well, what do you do it for?*

True, there are some external goods in freemasonry. In an earlier book, I wrote of the alchemy that:

… can take an ordinary chap and turn him into a Master of the Lodge: capable of running a meeting, making a speech, learning and delivering from memory a part in the ritual much the same length as 'Hamlet', and handling with aplomb such tricky words

---

[1] Harvard Business School Press, 2007.

as acquiescence, corporeal, immemorial and even parallelopipedon. [Freemasonry] enables everyone to shine, to take a place in the sun, to be recognised and congratulated and to feel good about themselves. [1]

These are external goods because such skills have a value external to freemasonry. In principle at least, a man might gain them by attending classes on public speaking, networking and the English language. There are other external goods: medical help, financial support when down on one's luck, loans of equipment to make ageing more bearable and a room in a masonic home when one can no longer manage on one's own. There is no doubt that these have a value and no doubt at all that we value them.

Nevertheless, these external goods are entirely incidental to the real and *internal goods* of freemasonry. The practice of freemasonry is about gains which can be recognised only by participating in the practice.

- It is wonderful when a shy brother blossoms but the internal good is the *wonder*, the fact that we find it wonderful.
- The efforts of the Preceptor may result in applause but that is incidental to his efforts: his efforts are *an expression of brotherly love*.
- When the ritual is done well, it is *a gift* to the lodge and to the candidate.
- On entering a lodge, the mason feels the *warmth of brotherhood*, the fact that everyone there *cares* for him.

The internal goods are the *wonder*, the *expression*, the *gift*, and the *warmth*, none of which have any external value nor could they be recognised or valued by anyone who is not a freemason. Such internal goods are simply not available to, and have no meaning for a non-mason, or a freemason who joined for the wrong, external reasons. Only a mason who understands freemasonry, and gives himself to it, would be able to experience them. Even to understand what I am saying requires you to be a good mason.

Practice and institution

MacIntyre argues that no practice *can survive for any length of time unsustained by an institution*, but practice and institution are different. The famous meeting of

---

[1] *The Goat, the Devil and the Freemason.*

the four lodges in 1717 turned out to be a decision to form an institution to govern the practice of freemasonry. One output of that decision was a *Book of Constitutions,* a book that is no more about the practice of freemasonry than the *Rules of Golf* are about the practice of golf.[1]

The *Rules* govern the manner in which golfers compete. They say nothing about how to hit a golf ball; nothing about how to read a putt and nothing about the joy of seeing a soaring 5 iron drop gracefully on the green. Few players actually compete. Oh, they may decide to play skins or stableford in their weekly four ball, but the result doesn't often matter. Most have forgotten the score a few seconds after (or even before) the end of the game. In the main, golfers enjoy their rounds with little or no reference to the rules, even making up their own as the occasion demands. Few go back to the tee to hit another when the first ball goes out of bounds. They would delay their partners and fellow club members if they did.

In a like manner, our *Constitutions* are largely about the external administration of freemasonry, about whether a lodge meeting should be abandoned (yes, if no Installed Master is present), adjourned (no) or cancelled (no); about the width of the collar of a Provincial Grand Steward (2.5 inches) or what happens if a brother has not paid his dues for two years (he is automatically excluded, although lodge treasurers will go to great lengths to avoid this, often at some cost to themselves). All this has almost nothing to do with the love of masonry.

Institutions should exist to facilitate the love of the practices they administer, but in owning property, managing investments, seeking and returning favours with other institutions, and maintaining a standing in the public world, institutions have a life of their own, much of which is unconnected with their purpose. Actions of an institution may well be contrary to the needs of the practice. Expenses can be racked up by entertainment of people the institution wishes to impress; the need to avoid public embarrassment may mean that a building is sold for far less than it is worth; the desire not to upset

---

[1] The great Patrick Campbell said that golf is the only game in which an excellent knowledge of the rules earns one a reputation for bad sportsmanship.

another institution may result in a description of the practice as less significant than it is; the desire for public recognition may result in PR becoming central to decision making. MacIntyre writes: [1]

> *Institutions are characteristically and necessarily concerned with what I have called external goods. They are involved in acquiring money and other material goods; they are structured in terms of power and status, and they distribute money, power and status as rewards.*

A corrupting power

The institution may offer external goods in exchange for behaviours protective of itself. MacIntyre calls this the *corrupting power* of the institution. A grand lodge may offer honours which motivate behaviours at variance to the practice. Instead of brotherly love, we may see competition; instead of alms motivated by love, we see charity collected as 'points' towards honours; instead of equality, we see courtship of those with the power to grant them. At Installed Masters' Lodges and other places where the hierarchy gathers, many masons will have experienced the attempt to hold a conversation with a brother who is looking around for others more important to them in their search for such honours.

The offer of external goods provides control, but the power of patronage creates dangers. It may prevent difficult messages being communicated upwards; filter out new ideas deemed unacceptable to the powerful, and disable disagreement. Many problems persist in organisations because people are not willing to tell the Emperor that he is wearing no clothes.

Motivation

Motivation is a massive subject, but the aspect most relevant for us is the distinction between intrinsic motivation *(motivation to complete a task for its own sake)* and extrinsic motivation *(motivation to complete a task for reward.)* Edward L. Deci reports findings that:

> *... contingent tangible rewards and other extrinsic factors such as competition and evaluations can be detrimental to outcomes such as creativity, cognitive flexibility, and*

[1] *After Virtue.*

problem solving, which has been found to be associated with intrinsic motivation …[1]

It is to intrinsic motivation that we appeal, to the love that the brethren have for freemasonry. We make a mistake in thinking that brethren will respond only to extrinsic motivation. The pretty jewels and grand titles, to show how much brethren and lodges have given to charity, are dangerous. Extrinsic motivation is often, and indeed usually, the victim of the law of unintended consequences. We have seen this in the health service where target setting has caused statistics to be falsified and in education where it has caused teachers to cheat over students' exam results, in each case to make it appear that targets have been reached when they had not.

The most significant danger with extrinsic motivation is that it reduces intrinsic motivation. Poor management has seen the extrinsic drive out the intrinsic even where the latter should be most powerful. People have been drawn to jobs in health and education traditionally by a desire to do something worthwhile, but nurses and teachers have found that achieving non-professional outcomes, and making things sound good when they are not, is the route to promotion. Such a disconnect is now causing a haemorrhage of talent in both professions.

Promotion to grand rank is the main extrinsic motivation in freemasonry and it has to be used with very great care, if it is not to cause similar damage our order. Promotion shows what we value and every wrong promotion is a slap in the face of the practice. A way to reduce the damage is to increase the number of grand officers, to double or treble the number, just as the way to reduce the cost of houses is to build more of them.

A new paradigm

Management has undergone considerable change since the Second World War, during which the US government undertook research to find ways of getting things done better and faster. In the first half of the 20th century, the management paradigm included 'facts' such as:

---

[1] *Intrinsic Motivation*, Plenum Press, 1975. See also 'Self-determination theory and work motivation', *Journal of Organizational Behaviour*, 2005.

Control must be maintained at all times.
Decisions must be made at the top and cascaded down.
Communication must follow the chain of command.
Obedience is due from the lower level to the upper level.

I dare say that these beliefs are still taken as common sense in many places today. Nevertheless, research into management has shown that while such beliefs may be common but they are not sense. Excellence in management has switched to a new paradigm, that:

Control is a matter of shared vision.
Creativity and imagination are more important than respecting a chain of command.
Empowerment matters more than obedience.
Ethics are critical parts of decision-making.

On the next page is a short questionnaire. Give it a go. It is not psychometric.[1] It is just a thought starter, or even a discussion starter.

---

[1] That is to say, the results cannot be taken as psychological truths about yourself.

Choose <u>one</u> statement (left or right) from each pair.

Freemasonry ought to:

Promote known brethren	Search for brethren to promote
Control what brethren may say	Encourage free speech
Keep disagreement private	Let dissent flourish
Re-appoint	Change to improve
Promote by seniority	Create a meritocracy
Centralise	Decentralise
Be careful what you say	Be honest and open
Maintain strong central governance	Use the centre as support function
Restrict decisions to the hierarchy	Get everyone involved
Marginalise misfits	Praise misfits
Do what makes us look good	Do what we think is right
Strive for uniformity	Prize local creativity
Observe best practices	Seek new practices
Honour tradition	Welcome the future
Put control first	Put action first
Create obedience	Create excitement
Keep costs down	Invest in growth

Count the statements you have chosen in each column.[1]

---

[1] Modified from Tom Peters, *Liberation Management*, Ballantine Books, 1995.

The more you choose *left-hand* statements, the more you may favour *control*, and the more you choose *right-hand* statements, the more you favour *change*.

Score	
14-17 left	You are a traditionalist, valuing control.
14-17 right	You are a change agent, valuing experiment.
11–13 left	You favour tradition but are open to ideas.
11–13 right	You are open to change but have a few sacred cows.
9-10 left	You are undecided but if pushed favour control.
9-10 right	You are undecided but if pushed favour change.

How would the brethren of your lodge score? Would they be traditionalists, change agents, or undecideds? We do need new ideas but we cannot command creativity, only encourage it to flourish. Creativity requires the establishment of a culture in which lateral thinking is normal, accepted, encouraged and supported. New ideas should not need a dispensation.

Management theory and brotherly love

Schön argued that it is in the nature of organisations to seek a stable state. Most demonstrate what he called dynamic conservatism: an active struggle to remain the same, despite change occurring all around them. My colleague and OD practitioner Professor Robin Stuart-Kotze has said:

Up to the middle of the 20th century, the economic environment in the Western world had remained relatively stable, arguably since Victorian times – stable in the sense of steady growth (barring periodic and temporary depressions), steady progression of technology and steady increase of knowledge. A relatively stable environment is compatible with stewardship which aims to keep things on course, maintain consistency, protect the investment in procedures and systems, and make things run as they were designed to run. However, as the pace of change quickened and unpredictability became normal in all walks of life, it became clear to some, that new behaviours were necessary. Managing the changing, the unknown, and the unpredictable requires vision and leadership. Leadership behaviour is about doing things differently. One tends to lead people and manage things.[1]

As Peter Senge writes, *the organisations who succeed now and in the future will be those that harness the imagination, spirit and intelligence of all their people,*[2] and what Jonas Ridderstråle and Kjell Nordstrom say about the modern knowledge organisation, bears keeping in mind:

The most critical resource wears shoes and walks out of the door 5 o'clock every day.[3]

In the knowledge organisation, the staff make the difference between success and failure. The knowledge workers are the only stock in trade and their commitment has to be maintained if the organisation is to prosper. This also applies to us. Our members do not have to stay, and unless we maintain their commitment and enthusiasm, they will leave. Harnessing the imagination, spirit and intelligence of all our brethren is not only a matter of brotherly love, it is also good management.

Good decisions are commonly the result of people becoming committed to making them work. If people support their leaders, are engaged with them, believe that they are doing their best, believe that their own efforts are respected and that they themselves are truly valued, then they will get behind decisions and make them come right.

So many decisions are taken emotionally. A character in Camus' *The Fall* says: *It hurts me to confess it, but I'd have given ten conversations with Einstein for an initial rendezvous with a pretty chorus girl.* We tend to ignore evidence contrary to our own opinions and exaggerate evidence in favour of them. Involvement acts as a brake upon decisions by subjecting them to the test of the opinions of others. Ridderstråle and Nordstrom write:

The boss is dead. No longer can we believe in a leader who claims to know more about everything and who is always right.[4]

---

[1] In conversation.

[2] *The Fifth Discipline*, Random House, revised edition 2006.

[3] *Op. cit.*

[4] *Ibid.*

Responsibility in successful companies is shared among the experts in one or more fields of knowledge and endeavour. Involvement is a sensible use of the resource available. In our lodges, we will almost certainly find the knowledge and skill needed in organisational development, change management, IT, social media, management development and leadership training. Autocracy disengages the brethren. Involvement is brotherly love.

Masonic leadership should exist to bring out the best in brethren; to develop, coach, facilitate, and communicate; to give the brethren a sense of achievement, and recognition; to offer responsibility and opportunities for personal growth. As Anita Roddick said:

> *There aren't many motivating forces more potent than giving your people an opportunity to exercise and express their idealism.* [1]

Research[2] shows that brethren will give more loyalty to leaders who are prepared to make sacrifices. That same research shows that a visible commitment to the brethren under their care is the most important asset a masonic leader can have. Interpersonal distance or demands for special treatment will dissipate loyalty. It should be obvious that the voluntary organisation needs a spirit of community and sense of mission. One of the most important phrases in management is *loose-tight*, as used by Peters and Waterman in their book, *In Search of Excellence*.[3] We must remain *tight* on our landmarks and values and on (a few) important rules but maintaining control is not an end in itself – nor is protecting anyone's ego.

Our aims can only be achieved with exemplary values, a culture of honesty and openness, an orientation towards achievement and a sense of ownership among all brethren. We need shared values, maximum trust and minimal controls. We need leadership that can capture hearts and minds, and instil the need for change. This demands *management by walking around* – in ordinary, private lodges as well as grand ones. Such leadership was not available in the nineteenth century but we cannot rely on serendipity again.

---

[1] *Business as Unusual*, Thorsons, 2000.

[2] For example, Mark van Vugt, 'Follow the leader', *The Psychologist*, 2004.

[3] Harper & Row, 1982.

Summary

The central message

There are periodic intervals in human experience when scientific, religious or economic events demand new ways of understanding moral relationships. During such upheavals, moral relativity seeks to take over. This time, it is our turn to respond. As freemasons, we must maintain a community in which the moral life is continued, even as it is lost elsewhere. We must be a moral stronghold, preserving the virtue of trust, a reservoir of social capital.

The world that we face now may seem less than welcoming to the ideals of freemasonry but there are large numbers of men in our society hungry for the fellowship and moral meaning that our institution offers. Our challenge is to bring our ideals to the attention of a new and very different audience. We know little about that audience and it will require hard work, open-mindedness, creativity and above all leadership to reach it. The optimism that runs through this book depends upon a willingness and an ability to change. Holding on to the past will be the last thing our order does.

History and society

* Membership has been in decline for over 60 years and the reversal of that trend will not be immediate.

* There is no pill we can take to make things better.

* Until we accept that the problem is systemic, we cannot solve it. Complacency is the enemy.

* Freemasonry is not isolated from society and effective management of our institution requires a grasp of what has been happening around us. It is not clear that this has consistently been achieved.

* We cannot understand the new audience for freemasonry, unless we understand the social changes that have given rise to it.

* The changes since the 1950s have made freemasonry unfashionable but in trying to reverse this, we have endangered our core values. In particular, we have neglected the fact that freemasonry is *a peculiar system*

of morality, veiled in allegory and illustrated by symbols. This is certainly not an empty phrase.

- Our secrets and rituals really do matter. The secrets satisfy a need for affiliation and create group cohesion. Our rituals teach important lessons. They are delivered *by* brethren, but also *for* brethren. The effort of learning and the perfection of delivery is a *gift* given by brother to brother. The practice of ritual is brotherly love in action. As Kirk C. White writes:

  Ritual causes mental change and that is its purpose … ritual accomplishes that change … by bracketing the time spent as 'special' and unlike our ordinary mundane lives … Our opening and closing rituals mark the time in lodge as different ...

- The nineteenth-century offers useful parallels with today. Freemasonry went into almost terminal decline and it was not until the serendipitous rise of the middle class that the decline was reversed.

- Facing unforeseen social and economic changes, freemasonry walked blindfold into a perfect storm with an almost complete lack of leadership. History is now repeating itself and we cannot rely on serendipity again.

Middle class

- For one hundred years, the middle class provided our candidates. As a recruitment source, it could not have been bettered, but it became habit forming. We were hooked on it as the source of candidates. We must now recognise that the middle class has gone away.

- The continuity and predictability which characterised middle class life no longer applies. We now see employment conditions reminiscent of the pre-Victorian era: pay often below a living wage, high unemployment and underemployment, longer working hours for less money, fear of redundancy, disappearance of job security and the end of the career.

- There are a few signs of hope today.

- Brethren and candidates now have less control over their time. Zero-hours contracts and increased 'self-employment' mean that many do not know when, or indeed if, they will work the following week.

- Lacking the ability to plan ahead, they cannot easily commit to attending meetings, even give notice of their intentions.
- The often-heard Past Master's remark, *When I was initiated …* has no relevance today.

Management

- Respect for and trust in senior management is at an all time low.
- The establishment has shown that it cannot be trusted.
- Work has lost its meaning and job satisfaction is at an all-time low.
- We must demonstrate we are different: that our senior management does understand the conditions of the ordinary masons; that it not only is ready to listen to their views but actively seeks them; that it does not reward itself in ways that contrast badly with the experience of the ordinary mason; that it is not a mutually congratulatory clique isolated from reality and that it does deserve the salutes and ovations it is given.
- Our leadership must demonstrate that morality matters and that in all our actions we place moral considerations first. This goes not just for crimes but also for the sins of arrogance, pride and self-aggrandisement.

Positive statement

- The false gods of PR push us in the wrong direction. In seeking to be accepted by the popular world, we have tried to portray freemasonry as a harmless, if eccentric, hobby.
- If we were to be successful in this, we might (but probably would not) gain acceptance in the popular world, but at the expense of our reason for being.
- We would lose those who seek meaning, purpose and the moral life.
- We need a clear and positive trumpet call to show what freemasonry is and what we stand for.
- Given such a statement, the public can agree or disagree with us, but at least they will not rely on gossip, rumour or slander for information.

Author with brethren of St George's Lodge No. 20, Grand Lodge of Nova Scotia

Our role

- We are a guardian of trust and a reservoir of social capital. We enable men to trust others and to be worthy of trust, virtues that are in decline in the popular world.

- Freemasonry offers a purpose-to-life from which moral virtues can be derived.

- Our order is one of the few communities able to sustain the moral life in an amoral world.

- Safeguarding the moral life is the main function of our order and our greatest challenge.

- We must become a bastion for the virtues, and thereby save ourselves.

- On a parallel with the Rule of St Benedict, a man must choose to be a freemason and in doing so commit himself to excellences by which to live: a life governed by the principles of brotherly love, relief and truth.

- There is no sense in which a man can say *I want to be a freemason but not a good one* because freemasonry is a moral practice.

Engineering

- The revitalisation of masonry is not a matter of tinkering with the periphery of our order.

- Only by focusing on the meaning of freemasonry, can we reverse the trend of membership.

- The analogy drawn in the book is of the commercial organisation that focuses on profit and thereby fails. It has forgotten that profit is the reward, not the product itself.

- Tinkering obscures the need for engineering.

Excellences of freemasonry

- *The Five Points of Fellowship* are of supreme importance. To live by the five points is to be trustworthy. To act upon them is to trust.

- The five points indicate a personal relationship between masons.

- Brotherly love may be partly defined by the phrase *all in it together*. Being brothers, we cannot pick and choose when to take sides.

- The word we use is *relief*, not philanthropy. The target of relief is an individual.

- Relief may be about money but it is equally about behaviour, acting from the heart.

- Given the issues that we face today, the original meaning of relief is more important than ever.

- Giving for political or PR reasons is not giving alms.

- A *true* mason is unfeigning and genuine: true to our ideals, a true and constant friend whose love of his brethren is truly demonstrated. Being true to each other, masons set an example in society. The masonic word *truth* connotes loyalty, legitimacy and fidelity.

- *Let prudence direct you* is an instruction to use reason and logic, and be open to advice.

- *Fortitude* is about maintaining our principles in the face of threat or persuasion.

- *Temperance* calls us to a life managed by reason, resisting temptation while experiencing human desires and feelings.

- A *just* action is one that is tested for impartiality, made without fear of popular opinion, unmotivated by hope of personal reward and positively consistent with our principles.

- The decencies of a Victorian gentleman are generally admired.

- We do not expect supererogation of ourselves. We are not an order of saints and heroes, but of ordinary men with responsibilities and ties, doing our best.

Practice and institution

- In difficult times we need more leadership visibility, not less.

- If a gulf opens between the worries of the ordinary private lodge and the concerns of those wearing chains, we shall find it nigh on impossible to turn things around.

- There is always a tension between *institution* and *practice.*.

- The power of patronage would not lightly be given up but we can reduce the damage by doubling the number of grand officers, just as to reduce the cost of houses we should build more.

- The desire for honours prevents difficult messages being communicated upwards, filters out new ideas deemed unacceptable to the powerful, and disables disagreement.

- Many problems persist in organisations because people are unwilling to tell the Emperor he is wearing no clothes.

- Honours are external goods, incidental to the practice of freemasonry, and often motivate behaviours at variance with it.

- Instead of brotherly love, we see competition; instead of alms motivated by love, we see charity collected as 'points' towards honours; instead of equality, we see courtship of those with the power to grant promotion.

Management and brotherly love

- Much of what happens in the modern organisation actively disengages its members.

- Given the poor state of management in the UK today, the audience we seek has little upward loyalty and has had its fill of autocracy.

- Our own management practices must be in tune with our professed values.

- We seek to create an organisation in which the spirit of community binds people together, where all brethren share a common mission and make extraordinary contributions to achieve it.

- Harnessing the imagination and intelligence of all brethren is both a matter of brotherly love and good management.

- Successful management, like a successful marriage, does not just happen. It needs to be worked at.

- Organisational learning starts with being honest about the gap between what we actually do and what we think we do.

Organisation culture

- Our aims can only be achieved by a sense of ownership among all brethren. If the brethren feel engaged and involved in decisions, they will get behind those decisions to make them come right.

- We need a culture in which lateral thinking is normal and actively encouraged.

- Control must be vested in a shared vision rather than in a hierarchy.

- Creativity and imagination are more important than a chain of command.

- Empowerment matters more than obedience and brotherly love is vital to decision-making.

- There is no correlation in our order between rank and the knowledge necessary to create such a community.

- Within our membership there will be skills in organisational development, change management, information technology, social media, training and organisation design.

- We should assemble a team of these experts to direct our change.

- We must train our future leaders in OD.

Recruitment

- Our members are now a declining source of candidates.

- Getting to know and evaluating the new audience requires more than a stilted committee meeting.

- The questions we ask in interviews describe a society which has ceased to exist.

- The relationship between the sexes has changed.

- Freemasons will continue to drink the loyal toast but the monarchy no longer warrants an interview question.

- No theologian accepts the *old man in the sky*. On the pattern of *Are you happy to drink the health of Her Majesty?* we should ask, *Are you happy to participate in prayers in lodge?*

A brief summary of the philosophical argument

- We cannot derive a moral statement (an *ought*) from a factual statement (an *is*) but moral judgements are more than expression of feelings.

- Sartre argues that to be *authentic*, a moral judgement implies an individual choice of *who to become*. In deciding that an action is acceptable, we choose to become a person who accepts such actions.

- That authentic moral judgement must be a rational act, not a matter of habit or obedience to uncritically accepted rules.

- The tradition of the virtues that stems from Aristotle does not start from facts. It assumes a purpose-to-life, the description of which is in itself a moral statement.

- Be careful with the term *purpose-to-life*. It is a technical term.

- It does not imply that there is only one purpose to life.

- *Life is all about* … is not a factual statement but a value judgement. It implies or discounts certain actions.

- The moral life is in danger today because it is almost impossible to find a context, a purpose-to-life, which can support it.

- The moral life will wither and decay, as in the *end of decency*.

- To be a Benedictine is to make an authentic choice to live by the Rule.

- On a parallel to the Rule of St Benedict, to be a freemason is to make an authentic choice to adopt our excellences.

- One cannot be a mason unless one lives by its principles One can only pretend to be one.

- Men seek a purpose-to-life in which the moral life finds traction.

- To provide it becomes our duty.

- It is also the way we will save ourselves.

Recommendations

The principles set out by Warren Bennis are still relevant:

Build trust. Maximise collaborative efforts. Increase a sense of ownership. Grow self-control and self-direction. Create an open, problem solving climate. Get decision-making and problem solving as close to the information sources as possible. Recognise the authority of knowledge and competence as opposed to rank.

Explain and propagate what we are, not what we are not

Make a 'big' statement of what we are.

Explain the internal goods of freemasonry.

Explain the nature and meaning of masonic virtues.

Be open to change

Accept the existence of the problem.

Stop making statements that all is well, when it isn't.

Study historical parallels.

Study the impact of social changes.

Recognise that we are a moral order

Empowerment matters more than obedience.

Make shared vision the only form of control.

Ensure that every decision is compatible with our principles.

Recognise that, like it or not, we now have a public, social duty.

The barbarian attacks on decency must be resisted.

Focus on the ordinary mason

Recognise his financial position.

Recognise the time demands on him.

Help older brethren understand the new audience.

Learn from successful lodges

Use the experience of successful lodges.

Identify what makes successful lodges work.

Twin successful lodges with less successful ones.

Create an open, problem solving climate

Involve the ordinary mason, not just the executive.

Explain proposed decisions before they are made.

Actively invite dissent, comment and questions.

Recognise the authority of knowledge as opposed to rank.

The phrase *distinctions among men* refers only to the ritual.

Reduce extrinsic motivation

Reduce the power of patronage.

Double or triple the number of Grand Officers.

Ensure that charity is given for the right motives.

Manage by walking about

Cease senior brethren's gatherings away from the ordinary mason.

Get members of the executive out to private lodges.

Look for talent in the order

Recognise that specialist know-how exists at all levels in our order.

Actively search for leadership potential among all brethren.

Promote only those capable of leadership.

Involve brethren in the appointment of the executive.

The future

The impact of the automation and AI revolution could well be as catastrophic as the industrial revolution.

We need to be planning our response now.

Additional points

Work with women's freemasonry to help them grow, and defuse accusations of misogyny.

Learn from women's freemasonry about feminism and freemasonry.

Learn from the Women's Institute how to support causes.

Complete the de-christianisation, especially of the Royal Arch.

List of illustrations

Bibliography

Alexander, Caroline, *The Endurance*, Bloomsbury, 1998.

Alfes, Kerstin *et al.*, *Creating an engaged workforce; findings from the Kingston employee engagement consortium project*, CIPD 2010.

Anderson, James, *The Constitutions of the Free-Masons*, 1723 & 1738, *Quatuor Coronati* facsimile edition 1976.

Andrews, Lyman, 'Lampedusa', *Fugitive Visions*, White Rabbit, 1962.

Anouilh, Jean, *Antigone*, Random House, 1946.

Aquinas, St Thomas
  Summa Theoligica, Ave Maria Press, 2000.
  Commentary the Nicomachean Ethics, tnsl. C.I. Litzinger OP, Henry Regnery Co., 1964.

Armstrong, *History of Freemasonry in Cheshire*, 1901.

Arndt, H.A., 'The Trickle-Down Myth', *Economic Development and Cultural Change*, Vol. 32, No. 1, 1983, The University of Chicago Press.

Barsacq, Jean-Louis, *Place Dancourt*, Gallimard, 2005.

Batham, C.N. (ed), *The Collected Prestonian Lectures 1961-1974*, Lewis Masonic, 1983.

Bennis, Warren, *Organizational Development*, Addison Wesley Longman, 1969.

Beresiner, Yasha, 'Robert Crucefix, a man and a mason to be proud of', *250th anniversary celebrations of Burlington Lodge*, 2006.

Bragg, Melvyn, *The Book of Books: the radical impact of the King James Bible, 1611-2011*, Hodder & Stoughton, 2011.

British Social Attitudes Survey, various years, Sage Publications.

Brown, Callum, *The Death of Christian Britain*, Routledge, 2001, 2nd edition 2009.

Brown, Richard, *Change and Continuity in British Society 1880–1850*, Cambridge, 1987.

Buck, Keith S, *Provincial Grand Lodge of Essex 1776–1976*, privately printed, 1976.

Busfield, Alan, 'The Last Forty Years of Freemasonry', *Proceedings of the United Masters Lodge No. 167*, Auckland, New Zealand, Vol. 26, 1986.

Byrne, Patrick, *The membership crisis in Freemasonry*, hinchley-wood-lodge.com.

Calderwood, Paul R., 'Architecture & Freemasonry in 20th-Century Britain', *AQC*, Vol. 126, 2013.

Chafe, William H, *The Unfinished Journey: America Since World War II*, Oxford University Press, 2006.

Catholic Church, *Compendium of the Catechism of the Catholic Church*, Libreria Editrice Vaticana, 2005.

Cleckley, Hervey, *The Mask of Sanity*, 1941, Literary Licensing LLC, 2011.

Dabney, Robert L, *Systematic Theology*, 1878, The Banner of Truth Trust, 1996.

Davies, Gareth, 'The Duke of Sussex lays a Foundation Stone,' *The Square*, June 2015.

Deci, Edward L.

Intrinsic Motivation, Plenum Press, 1975,

'Self-determination theory and work motivation', *Journal of Organizational Behaviour*, 2005.

Dixon, William, *Freemasonry in Lincolnshire*, 1894, Forgotten Books, 2014.

Doney, Keith

Freemasonry in France during the Nazi Occupation, Keith Doney, PhD Thesis for the University of Aston in Birmingham, May 1993.

'French Freemasonry and the Resistance 1940–1944', *Freemasonry Today*, April 2002.

Donne, John, 'Station 17, Now this bell tolling softly for another…', *Devotions upon Emergent Occasions and Death's Duel*, 1624, Vintage Spiritual Classics, 1999.

Dyer, Colin, *William Preston and his work*, Lewis Masonic, 1987.

Fine, Cordelia, *A Mind of its Own*, Icon Books, 2007.

Francis, Thomas, *History of Freemasonry in Sussex*, 1883, Forgotten Books, 2013.

Fraser, George MacDonald, *Quartered Safe Out Here*, HarperCollins, 1995.

Fryer, D. and Stambe, R., 'Neoliberal austerity and unemployment', *The Psychologist*, Vol.27, No 4, April 2014.

Fulford, Roger, *The Royal Dukes: the Father and Uncles of Queen Victoria*, Collins, 1973.

Gorbachev, Mikhail, *Perestroika*, Collins, 1987.

Gunn, Simon & Bell, Rachel, *Middle Classes: their rise and sprawl*, Cassell & Co, 2002.

Halpenny, Frances G. & Hamelin, Jean, *Dictionary of Canadian Biography*, Vol. 5, University of Toronto Press, 1983.

Hamel, Gary, *The Future of Management*, Harvard Business School Press, 2007.

Hammer, Andrew, *Observing the Craft*, Mindhive Books, 2010.

Han, Byung-Chul, *The Burnout Society*, Stanford University Press, 2015.

Hare, Robert D, *Psychopathy: Theory and Research*, John Wiley & Sons Inc., 1970.

Harrison, David, *The Transformation of Freemasonry*, Arima Publishing, 2010.

Henderson, Kent & Belton, John, 'Freemasons – An Endangered Species?', *AQC*, Vol. 113, 2000.

Herzberg, Frederick, *Motivation to Work*, John Wiley & Sons, 1959.

Hobbes, Thomas, *Leviathan, or The Matter, Forme and Power of a Common Wealth Ecclesiasticall and Civil*, 1651.

Hume, David, *Treatise of Human Nature*, 1738.

Jackson, A.C.F., *English Masonic Exposures 1760–1769*, Lewis Masonic, 1986.

James, P.R., 'The Grand-Mastership of HRH The Duke of Sussex, 1813–1843', *The Collected Prestonian Lectures 1961–1974*, Lewis Masonic, 1983.

Jones David M. & Molyneaux, Brian L., *Mythology of the American Nations*, Hermes House, 2009.

Kearsley, Mike, '1814 – Consolidation and Change', *AQC*, Vol. 127, 2014.

Keiningham, Timothy & Aksoy, Lerzan, *Why Managers Should Care about Employee Loyalty*, American Management Association, 2009.

Kellerman, Maurice, 'The Challenge of Changes in Membership in New South Wales', *Proceedings of the 1992 Australian Masonic Research Council Conference*.

Kennedy, Paul, *Rise and Fall of the Great Powers*, Random House, 1987.

King, Steven, *Poverty and welfare in England 1700–1850*, Manchester Univ. Press, 2000.

Knoop, Douglas *et al.*, *The Early Masonic Catechisms*, *Quatuor Coronati* Lodge, 1943.

Lane, John, *Masonic Records 1717-1894*, United Grand Lodge of England, 1895.

Larkin, Philip, 'This be the verse', *High Windows*, Faber & Faber, 1979.

Lewin, Kurt, 'Group decision and social change', in Newcomb, T. and Hartley, E. (eds), *Readings in social psychology*, Holt, 1947.

Lewis, C.S., *The Four Loves*, Geoffrey Bles, 1960.

Loftus, Donna, *The Rise of the Victorian Middle Class*, BBC History, 2011.

MacIntyre, Alasdair

    Dependent Rational Animals, Carus Publishing, 1999.

    After Virtue, University of Notre Dame Press, 2007.

Maslow, Abraham, 'A Theory of Human Motivation', *Psychological Review*, 1943.

Mason, Paul, *Post-capitalism: a guide to our future*, Allen Lane, 2015.

McGregor, Douglas, *The Human Side of Enterprise*, McGraw Hill, 1960.

McInnes, Tom et al., *Monitoring Poverty and Social Exclusion 2014*, Joseph Rowntree Foundation, 2014.

Mitchell, B.R., *British Historical Statistics*, Cambridge University Press, 1988.

Murray, Roy, 'The four cardinal virtues and the tassels in the lodge room', *AQC*, Vol. 107, 1999.

Murray, Will, *Corporate Denial*, Capstone Publishing, 2004.

Newman, John Henry, *Newman Reader*, The National Inst. for Newman Studies, 2007.

Nink, Marco, 'Employee Disengagement Plagues Germany', *Business Journal*, April 2009.

Noll, Thomas et al., 'A Comparison of Professional Traders and Psychopaths in a Simulated Non-Zero Sum Game', *Catalyst*, Vol. 2, Issue 2, 2012.

Nordström Kjell, and Ridderstråle, Jonas, *Funky Business*, Pearson, 2000.

Novak, Michael, *The Spirit of Democratic Capitalism*, Simon & Schuster, 1982.

Oliver, Dr George, *The Book of the Lodge*, 1864, The Aquarian Press, 1986.

Payne, Brian & Dorothy, *Extracts from the Journals of John Deakin Heaton, M.D. of Claremont, Leeds*, Publications of the Thoresby Society, Miscellany 1973, Vol. 15.

Peters, Thomas J.

    with Waterman, Robert H. Jnr, *In Search of Excellence*, Harper & Row, 1982.

    Thriving on Chaos, Macmillan, 1991.

    Liberation Management, Ballantine Books, 1995.

Pottinger, R, 'New Zealand Freemasonry in 2005', *Transactions of Masters and Past Masters Lodge No. 130*, Christchurch, New Zealand, 1997.

Price, Richard, *A Discourse on the Love of our Country*, The Constitution Society, 1789.

Putnam, Robert D., *Bowling Alone*, Simon & Schuster, 2000.

Rampton, Martha, 'The Three Waves of Feminism', *Pacific Magazine*, Fall 2008.

Raven, Simon, *Alms for Oblivion*, Vintage, 1998.

Richardson, Sarah, *The Domestic Impact of the Napoleonic Wars*, University of Warwick.

Ricks, Christopher (ed.), *Tennyson: A selected edition*, Longman, 1989.

Ridley, Jasper, *A Brief History of the Freemasons*, Robinson, 2008.

Riley-Smith, Jonathan, 'Revival and Survival', in Jonathan Riley-Smith (ed.) *The Oxford History of the Crusades*, Oxford University Press, 1999.

Roddick, Anita, *Business as Unusual*, Thorsons, 2000.

Sacks, Jonathan, *The Politics of Hope*, Random House, 1997.

Sandbach, R.S.E., 'Robert Thomas Crucefix 1788-1850', *AQC*, Vol. 102, 1989.

Sandel, Michael J., *Justice*, Allen Lane, 2009.

Scase, Richard and Goffee, Robert, *Reluctant Managers*, Routledge, 1989.

Schön, Donald

    Beyond the Stable State, Norton, 1973.

    with Argyris, Chris, *Theory in practice: Increasing professional effectiveness*, Jossey-Bass, 1974.

    with Argyris, Chris, *Organizational learning: A theory of action perspective*, Addison-Wesley, 1978.

Senge, Peter M., *The Fifth Discipline*, Random House, revised edition 2006.

Shelley, Percy Bysshe, '1819', in *Percy Bysshe Shelley*, poems selected by Fiona Sampson, Faber and Faber, 2011.

Smiley, Jane (ed.), *The Life and Death of Cormac the Skald*, Penguin Classics, 2001. (Written 1250–1300 CE, Icelandic author unknown.)

Social Issues Research Centre, *Future of Freemasonry*, 2012, A report for the United Grand Lodge of England.

Stevenson, Charles L., *Ethics and Language*, Yale University Press, 1944.

Stout, Martha, *The Sociopath Next Door*, Broadway Books, 2005.

Taylor, Frederick W., *Principles of Scientific Management*, Harper & Brothers, 1911.

Thatcher, Margaret, *The Downing Street Years*, HarperCollins, 1993.

Thompson, F.M.L. (ed), *The Rise of Suburbia*, Leicester University Press, 1982.

Thornton, Peter, 'Nine out of ten Freemasons would attack Moscow in Winter', *Proceedings of the 1992 Australian Masonic Research Council Conference*.

Tolkien, J.R.R., *Return of the King*, Allen & Unwin, 1955.

Trevelyan, G.M., *History of England*, Longman, illustrated edition 1973.

Vallance, Edward, *A Radical History of Britain*, Abacus, 2010.

Verschoor, Curtis C., 'New Survey of Workplace Ethics Shows Surprising Results', *AccountingWEB*, April 2012.

Vugt, Mark van, 'Follow the leader', *The Psychologist*, 2004.

Weil, Simone, *The Need for Roots*, Routledge & Kegan Paul, 1952.

West, David

    Employee Engagement - and the failure of leadership, Createspace, 2012.

    St Laurence Working (ed), privately published for St Laurence Lodge, No. 5511, stlaurencelodge.org.uk, 2010, second edition 2013.

    The Devil, the Goat and the Freemason - a study in the history of ideas, Hamilton House, 2013.

    Deism - at the time of the founders of the Premier Grand Lodge, Hamilton House, 2015.

    Things to do when you have nothing to do - never be short of candidates again, Hamilton House, 2014, second edition 2017.

    with Matthew West, *Masonic Legends*, Hamilton House, 2018.

White, Kirk C., *Operative Freemasonry: a manual for restoring light and vitality to the fraternity*, Five Gates Publishing, 2012.

Williams, Karel, *From Pauperism to Poverty*, Routledge and Kegan Paul, 1981.

Wilson, David, 'How psychopaths hide in plain sight – a psychological analysis of serial killer Dennis Rader', *Independent*, 18 August 2015.

Winn, Ray, *Running the Red: An Evaluation of Strathclyde Police's Red Light Camera Initiative - Research Findings*, The Scottish Government Publications, 1999.

Wittgenstein, Ludwig

    Tractatus Logico-Philosophicus, trnsl. D.F. Pears & B.F. McGuinness, Routledge, 1961.

    'Lecture on Ethics', from notes taken by Rush Rhees, *Philosophical Review*, Vol. 74, 1965.

    Philosophical Investigations, Basil Blackwell, 1967.

World Health Organization (*WHO*), *The Global Burden of Disease, 2004 Update*, 2008.

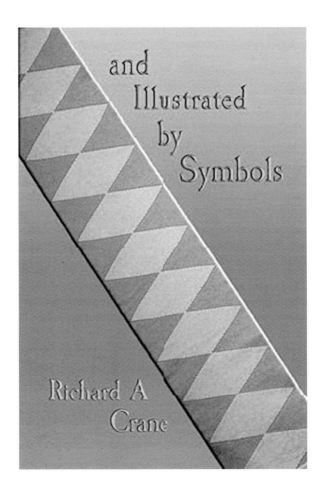

You will be familiar with the Royal Arch, **but do you truly understand it?** In this new book, Richard Crane distills the very essence of the order, and explains the significance of music, philosophy and religion to freemasonry.

Prestonian Lecturer and former Grand Treasurer for the Craft and Royal Arch, he is a man of many parts: an RAF navigator, a gifted musician, a captain of industry, academically qualified in music, philosophy and theology.

How come freemasonry's rituals are laced with scientific notions? Why the reliance on allegory? How did such a dubious group of founders create a brotherhood based on humanitarian principles and why did the beauty of the result outweigh their shortcomings?

Once in every generation there comes a lateral thinker who brings new perspectives to old questions. Professor Charles Lawrence is an internationally recognised scientist & engineer. He explains freemasonry using the same analysis and objectivity he applies to his scientific work. He raises questions not easily answered and not always palatable, but for those seeking a true *Key to Modern Freemasonry*, this book is invaluable.

Never be short of candidates again - SECOND EDITION

A stimulating account of how to turn your lodge around. New edition of the sell-out book, with even more things to do. Successful and practical. Has helped many lodges to turn decline into growth. Provides the scripts of things to do to add interest and excitement to your lodge.

Just add energy!

More books from Hamilton House Publishing
hamiltonhousepublishing.com

Alchemy still exerts a fascination and in this book Bob Black, an acknowledged expert on the subject, provides a serious but not overly academic introduction, including papers read to the *Rosicrucian Society* on the development of alchemy from the earliest times, featuring individual alchemists from Plato to the fascinatingly mysterious Fulcanelli.

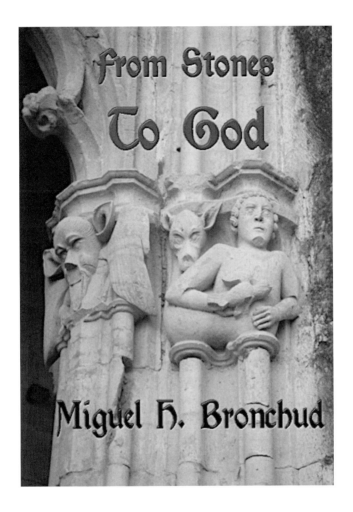

A traveller's guide to master builders. Catalonian oncologist and author, Miguel Hernández Bronchud, describes tours for you to take in England, Spain, Rhodes, Italy and France. With its hundreds of original photos, his unique book will enable you to plan trips, short or long, exploring the mystical energies of Spanish Templar castles, the chiaroscuro of Spanish and English cathedrals, the city walls of Avignon, Rome and Rhodes, and the architectural wonders of Barcelona. He describes the art and hidden knowledge of the Knights Templar and, the Knights of St John, as well as the life and works of three master builders: Reinard des Fonol, Don Juan Fernández de Heredia and the modern Antoni Gaudí.

The truth about the legends. You know about King Solomon and the Queen of Sheba, and quite possibly about Athelstan and Prince Edwin. But do you know how the prince is connected with industrial relations? Or what the queen has to do with air freight? What do you know about the Assyrians? How about the tale of David the Bandit or how bad Jezebel really was? Do you have any idea when the first temple was built or how historically accurate is Exodus? Did you know that there are 300 lodges and 30,000 masons in Cuba? Have you ever heard of José Martí, Bernardo O'Higgins, or the great Belgrano (the man not the ship)? Have you ever wondered why Rudyard Kipling so rarely attended lodge, and who on earth was Hobbehod?

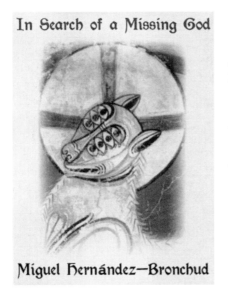

A search for meaning and for hope; a search for a God who seems to have hidden himself away, or whom we have lost. Where to look? Miguel Hernández Bronchud leads the way.

A study in the history of ideas. How did a goat become associated with freemasonry? Why do devils look like goats? How did goats become bad? What do you know about Albert Pike, Éliphas Lévi, Eusebius and Pan? How are the ram-headed gods of Egypt connected? What has masonry to do with the Comanche and the Wild West? David West gives us a wide-ranging history tour.

A concise introduction to a movement, very important to the early development of freemasonry. Philosopher David West explains what it was, how it differed from mainstream Christianity, and why it attracted our founders.

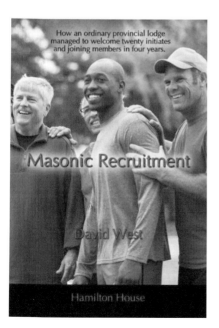

A short and practical 'how to' book, summarising the successful St Laurence Lodge method of recruitment; so successful, it had to close its waiting list for three years.